A History of *The Freeman*

# A History of *The Freeman*

LITERARY LANDMARK
OF THE EARLY TWENTIES

by Susan J. Turner

*Columbia University Press*
New York and London 1963

Susan J. Turner, who received her Ph.D. degree
from Columbia University in 1956, is Professor of English
at Vassar College.

Copyright © 1956, 1963 Columbia University Press
First published in book form in 1963
Library of Congress Catalog Card Number: 63-19075
Manufactured in the United States of America

# Preface

A sign of the vitality of the early 1920s in America was the brilliance, range, and intellectual "seriousness" to be found in the pages of the advanced magazines of the period. The *Freeman*, a weekly journal of politics and the arts, established in New York in the first year of the decade, was one of these. "Designed," as its prospectus said, "to meet the new sense of responsibility and the new spirit of inquiry" which the post-war world had "liberated," the *Freeman*, like the new *Dial*, the *Nation*, and the *New Republic*, in whose company it can best be described, exerted a solid share of influence on the intellectual life of a wonderfully creative time in our cultural history.

During that period the intellectual awakening which gave us our sense of the modern was in full swing. We recognize it as an international phenomenon, yet we know that in America it took a particular form. Ezra Pound, seeing his country freshly after a stay abroad, had predicted a risorgimento in 1912 and had described its scope and aspirations. It was "to have its effect not only in the arts, but in life, in politics, and in economics"; it implied "a whole volley of liberations; liberations from ideas, from stupidities, from conditions and from tyrannies of wealth or army." Pound's prophecy, with its implication that an organic relationship between society and the arts would substantiate both man's freedom and the growth of his intellect, reaffirmed for the twentieth century what Emerson had declared for the nineteenth. And this prophesy, like Emerson's, was expressive of the energies which a critic of imagination could see latent in a seemingly sterile society. American writers other than Pound, notably Van Wyck Brooks, were also to sense and to focus these energies during the prewar years. Although the war interrupted clear manifestations that a renaissance had begun, the conflict and its aftermath, with the attendant despair about civilization, caused, paradoxically, an intensified hope that regeneration was possible. This temper is reflected constantly in the advanced magazines of 1920. Indeed, to be an advanced magazine at that time meant to support in one form or another the aims of the risorgimento and to interpret the very real evidence, in the arts and sciences at least, that liberations had come.

The challenge to the critic was a vigorous one, demanding far more power than the old genteel critical mode could provide—genuine shifts in language and sensibility as well as in beliefs about tradition and society. To examine the course of advanced criticism in the periodicals of the early twenties is to find, clearly, the roots of modern taste. But it is to find also, after a brief time, a growing division in critical attitudes that diminishes, for an understanding of society and the arts, the broad, humane view of the imagination suggested in Pound's vision of a risorgimento.

The origins of the *Freeman*, its behavior, and its point of view place it in a distinctive relationship to these formative years. (It was published from 1920 to 1924.) My main concern in this study of the magazine is with the literary criticism, seen not dryly as the formulation of critical theory alone, but as a constant activity, a criticism composed in passion, conviction and controversy by writers responding day by day to the cultural and political life around them. Understanding this activity meant, I found, giving attention to the history of the magazine, to the persons who edited it and wrote for it, and to its meaning for its age. In so presenting the *Freeman*, I have sought not only to revive the memory of an excellent journal of opinion but also to illuminate four years of the twenties which have been dimmed by the radiance of the decade as a whole.

During the course of my investigation of the *Freeman*, I

became indebted, through interviews and correspondence, to the following men and women who were connected with the magazine or who knew members of the editorial staff: the late Van Wyck Brooks, Mrs. Francis Dixon (Emilie McMillan), Miss Suzanne La Follette, Mr. B. W. Huebsch, Professor Francis J. Nock, Professor Geroid T. Robinson, Miss Ruth Robinson, Miss Catherine Wilson, and Mrs. Eric Woolson (Lucie Taussig). They gave me, with great liberality and courtesy, information concerning the *Freeman*. My use of this information and the inferences I have drawn from it are, I should stress, entirely my own.

I wish gratefully to acknowledge a Faculty Fellowship from Vassar, which provided me with time for research and writing. And I want to thank the friends and colleagues there and elsewhere who gave me advice and encouragement during my work on the *Freeman* and its period. I cannot name them all, but I should like to thank particularly John Cutler, Ruth Elson, Elizabeth Hardwick, and Caroline Mercer for reading parts or the whole of the manuscript and for their aid in matters of intellectual history or literary criticism. I want also to thank Charles Griffin for reading the chapter on politics, Ida Treat for her accounts of the journalism of the early twenties, and William Rose, Catherine Lindsay, and J. B. Ross for editorial suggestions. Members of the staff of the Vassar College Library, where I did much of the writing and checking, have been unfailingly cooperative.

Josephine Gleason's scrutiny of the book—content, style, and footnotes—in its preparation for the publisher has been invaluable.

Lastly, I owe a very great debt to Jacques Barzun and Lionel Trilling, under whom I studied at Columbia University some years ago. They have continued to take an active and generous interest in my work.

A grant from the Lucy Maynard Salmon Fund at Vassar

College has helped to make possible the publication of this book.

SUSAN J. TURNER

*Poughkeepsie, New York*
*July 12, 1963*

# Permissions

I am pleased to acknowledge the gracious permission of the following publishers and individuals to quote passages from the books listed below.

E. P. Dutton: *Days of the Phoenix, Scenes and Portraits, Sketches in Criticism,* and *Three Essays on America* (including *America's Coming-of-Age* and *Letters and Leadership,* which were originally published by B. W. Huebsch), by Van Wyck Brooks

Harcourt, Brace and World: *Fighting Years,* by Oswald Garrison Villard; "Radicalism," by George Soule, in *Civilization in the United States: An Inquiry by Thirty Americans,* edited by Harold E. Stearns

Harper and Row: *Memoirs of a Superfluous Man,* by Albert Jay Nock

The Hogarth Press: *Autobiography,* by Edwin Muir

Ralph Fletcher Seymour: *Patria Mia,* by Ezra Pound

The Viking Press: *The Freeman Book; Latitudes,* by Edwin Muir

Miss Edna Bryner: *Man Seen* and *Port of New York,* by Paul Rosenfeld

Miss K. P. Evans and C. G. Nelson (publishers): *My Life in Two Worlds,* by Francis Neilson

# Contents

# A History of *The Freeman*

## Chapter One

# The Founding of *The Freeman*

The founding of the *Freeman* was the result of that familiar conjunction of wealth and social conscience, of plutocracy and the arts, so often characteristic of our liberal institutions. Many other leading intellectual magazines of the twenties were established in this same way. Rich persons backed the *Nation*, the *New Republic*, the *Dial* and the *Freeman* in order to foster critical views on certain aspects of American life. In each case the sponsors of these magazines were committing themselves to a project which engaged their imaginations or even involved their active participation. A railway magnate, Henry Villard, wishing to contribute to the cause of a free press in America,[1] bought the *Nation* in 1881, kept it in the family, and willed it to his son, who became the editor some thirty years later. Willard Straight's desire to influence public opinion and his deep interest in Herbert Croly's *The Promise of American Life* were responsible for the founding of the *New Republic* in 1914 as a means of applying to current issues "the political and social ideas . . . sketched in the book." [2] And, in the field of the arts, Scofield Thayer and John Sibley Watson, two wealthy young Harvard aesthetes, did journeyman's work on the new *Dial*, which they financed and reorganized in 1920.[3] It was also in this year that the *Freeman*, sponsored by the Swift packing fortune of Chicago, was founded—the last of four periodicals which formed the leadership of advanced opinion in the United States at the turn of the decade. The gift of a fabulously rich woman to her husband, who was a poor man,

1. Villard, *Memoirs*, II, 338–39.
2. Croly, *Willard Straight*, p. 472.
3. Hoffman *et al.*, *The Little Magazine*, pp. 196–204.

an intellectual, an agrarian radical, the *Freeman* seems the most merchant-princely and the most American of them all.

The autobiographies and letters of the two founding editors and the reminiscences of others connected with the magazine, together with the memoirs and letters of figures in the intellectual world of the twenties, provide sufficient material for a summary of the events—personal, cultural, and political—which brought the *Freeman* into being.

In the autumn of 1912 Mrs. Helen Swift Neilson, formerly Mrs. Edward Morris, decided to found a new magazine to express the political views of her second husband, Francis Neilson. She had tried the year before, her husband tells us, to buy the *Nation* for that purpose, but Oswald Garrison Villard had refused her offer.[4] Neilson also tells us that the suggestion for the founding of the *Freeman* came from Albert Jay Nock, who was then an American journalist identified with the Steffens-Tarbell "liberal crowd" and a former editor of the *American Magazine*. Neilson, an Englishman, was, too, a writer and a reformer, a man of wider experience than Nock, and, from 1910 to 1915, a Liberal member of Parliament and an ardent advocate of land reform. It was partly at Nock's instigation that Neilson, at odds with the Liberals and financially unsettled, had moved to America in 1915, where he lectured as a political analyst until his marriage to Helen Swift Morris in 1917.

The reform era, facing the exigencies of the world war that was to bring it to a close, shaped the circumstances by which Francis Neilson and Albert Jay Nock became acquainted. They were brought together in the spring of 1915 by their common friend, Brand Whitlock, who was then serving as United States Minister to Belgium.[5] Both men had become intimate

4. Neilson, *My Life in Two Worlds*, II, 41.
5. Neilson, *The Story of "The Freeman,"* pp. 4–7. This pamphlet and also Neilson's accounts of the *Freeman* in his autobiography are colored

with Whitlock through their affiliation with the single-tax movement: Nock had worked with him during Whitlock's term as Progressive Mayor of Toledo; Neilson, having met Whitlock on an ocean crossing in 1912, had introduced him to certain political figures in England who were committed to furthering the land policy within the Liberal party. Three years later, in the first spring of the war, Nock, operating abroad as an unofficial emissary of William Jennings Bryan, applied to Whitlock for information that might be of use to the State Department. Knowing that Neilson, disaffected with his party, was at work in England on a book exposing the imperialist diplomacy of the Liberals, Whitlock gave Nock a letter of introduction to this dissident member of Parliament. One result of their meeting was that Nock took Neilson's manuscript, *How Diplomats Make War*, back to America for publication; another, that they became friends, drawn together by their common political convictions and, it seems, by a sense that in a world of missions, diplomatic secrets, changing reputations, and great causes they might be of use to each other.

At the time of this meeting in 1915, Neilson was forty-eight and Nock was forty-two; their characters had crystallized, and the stamp of their experience was upon them. Different as they were in personality, intellect, and background, they were idealists whose habits of mind had been formed by many of the same influences. Both had grown to political consciousness at the end of the nineteenth century and had responded to the same kinds of political protest in the reform era. Both had done professional service in the single-tax cause. Both had a strong

---

by the bitterness which the author felt toward Nock during the course of their association on the *Freeman*. The material as a whole is the fullest, most concrete account we have of the founding of the magazine; Nock's memoirs treat the *Freeman* from the date of its actual appearance in 1920 and do not mention persons by name. Only a few of Nock's letters about the *Freeman* are extant, apparently. See Introduction to *Selected Letters of Albert Jay Nock*, written by his son, Francis J. Nock.

distrust of parliamentary governments, and both believed that such governments were the cause of an imperialist war which they hated. These were strong bonds to cement their friendship, and, in addition, the war had wrought a situation which made their careers potentially complementary.

At the core of their political beliefs was the program of Henry George, at the time of their young manhood a potent ideology. John Chamberlain has called that period a "crazy-quilt pattern" of political discontent. In those years, as he says, when "the nineteenth century merged into the twentieth," radicalism

looked back to Jefferson and Jackson; it looked across the ocean to the primitive communism of Tolstoy; it dallied with De Leonism, an intransigent brand of socialism . . . even looked forward to no government at all, following Kropotkin and the anarchists.[6]

George's protest against poverty and landed monopoly, registered in *Progress and Poverty* (1879), had struck the imaginations of reformers of many kinds, attracting those who leaned toward the socialist state and those who found in George a hope of securing economic justice without destroying the liberal belief of the early nineteenth century that the government is best which governs least. In itself a composite of various strains of social thought, George's program was based on a theory of natural rights, an agrarian economy, and the free competition posited by classical economic liberalism. Accepting the framework of the capitalist system, George had proposed a fiscal policy designed to strike at the heart of economic privilege as he saw it in his day, especially in America. For him the possession of a country's land by a few private owners, when he believed that its value had actually been determined by the whole of society, seemed the key to all social injustice.[7] The

6. Chamberlain, *Farewell to Reform*, p. 42.

7. Taken in part from Grimes, *The Political Liberalism of the New York "Nation,"* p. 22.

confiscation not of the land itself but of its unearned increment (its economic rent) would, he reasoned, free the land from monopoly control and provide sufficient government revenue to release savings from other taxes for the benefit of the whole economy. Beyond this releasing of economic energy for the good of a people lay—Utopia. Summarizing his theory in his preface to the fourth edition of *Progress and Poverty*, George had described it thus:

It is seen that private property in land, instead of being neces-sary to its improvement and use, stands in the way of improvement and use, and entails an enormous waste of productive forces; that the recognition of the common right to land involves no shock or dispossession, but is to be reached by the simple and easy method of abolishing all taxation save that upon land values. . . .

A consideration of the effects of change proposed then shows that it would enormously increase production; would secure justice in distribution; would benefit all classes; and would make possible an advance to a higher and nobler civilization. . . .

The law of human progress shows . . . that differences in civili-zation are not due to differences in individuals, but rather to dif-ferences in social organization; that progress, always kindled by association, always passes into retrogression as inequality is de-veloped; and that even now, in modern civilization, the causes which have destroyed all previous civilizations are beginning to manifest themselves, and that mere political democracy is running its course toward anarchy and despotism. But it also identifies the law of social life with the great moral law of justice, and . . . shows how retrogression may be prevented and a grander advance begun.[8]

This statement, with its evocation of "the great moral law of justice" and the surging of social idealism against the dry factuality of the theory, suggests the quality of *Progress and Poverty* which so impressed George's contemporaries. John Jay Chapman, for example, called the final chapter of the book,

8. George, "Preface to the Fourth Edition," *Progress and Poverty*, p. xvi.

where [George] gets to describing the New Jerusalem of the Single Tax . . . a romance—a rhapsody—a vision—at the end of a long seeming scientific discussion of rent, interest, and wages. . . . This burst of song, being the only lyric poetry of this commercial period, is popular.[9]

It is not surprising that, in spreading from America to England and the Continent, the power of the single-tax radicalism which George inspired lay as much in its moral conviction as in its fiscal policy. Strains of this radicalism were incorporated into the principles of the Liberal party in England and became part of the whole progressive ethos in the United States, influencing the muckrakers and inspiring at least one American millionaire, Joseph Fels, to devote most of his fortune and the last ten years of his life to propagandizing the single tax.[10] Thus, either as political dogma or as a state of mind, the philosophy of George had inspired reformers for over thirty years, from the publication of *Progress and Poverty* in 1879 until the First World War. The international character of the single-tax movement, its part in the Liberal Land Bills of 1909–10, the philanthropy of Joseph Fels and his League for the Taxation of Land Values, the fact that many of the muckrakers were Georgists— all had an influence on the founding of the *Freeman*.

Although their association with the Georgist movement was doubtless the strongest political link between Francis Neilson and Albert Jay Nock in 1915, there was also a congeniality in their views about the state as an instrument of power in the

9. M. A. de Wolfe Howe, ed., *John Jay Chapman and His Letters*, p. 174.

10. Joseph Fels was the manufacturer of Fels-Naptha Soap. The dedication of this industrialist to economic reform greatly impressed the muckrakers. Lincoln Steffens, describing a speech Fels made to an audience of meat packers and other men of great wealth in Chicago, reports that he said: "We can't get rich under present conditions without robbing somebody. I've done it; you are doing it now and I am still doing it. But I am proposing to spend the damnable money to wipe out the system by which I made it." Quoted in Steffens, "Interesting People: Joseph Fels," *American Magazine*, LXX (Oct., 1910), 744–45.

hands of a predatory class, blocking economic emancipation and individual liberty. A form of philosophical anarchism, their belief belonged to the historico-sociological theories of the state current at the time and to the whole feeling about "privilege" which was consonant with George's hopes for the decline of "mere political democracy" and with the discoveries of the muckrakers about the economic nature of political power. It is impossible to say just what, in the way of a tradition, was contributed by each man to the formation of the idea of the state that was to animate the *Freeman*. Neilson, who wrote *The Old Freedom* in 1919, identified his theories with Herbert Spencer and with what he called the English radical tradition, from Paine through the philosophical radicals to Cobden and Bright and then to his own radical branch of the Liberal party. Nock looked back to individualist Jeffersonian principles. Both saw a relation between their theories of the state and the wrongness of the war which was the work of "the office-holders," of the "machinations and misfeasances of a baker's dozen of men who by deviltry and chicane and compromise and all the devious ways of the professional 'statesman' get into office and make up governments," as Nock said of them in his preface to *How Diplomats Make War*. This book, he continued, expressing his own and Neilson's pacifism,

is no . . . cheap and empty partisan effort. It shifts our sympathies squarely away from the whole brawling gang of governments— the whole intolerable system of orthodox statecraft, wherever practiced—the whole filthy prairie-dog's nest of traditional diplomacy, wherever found—and seeks to fix it on the deceived, hoodwinked and inarticulate people of all countries alike; people who have no ghost of a quarrel with one another and ask nothing better than to be let alone.[11]

Francis Neilson has recorded the development of his politics in an autobiography, *My Life in Two Worlds*, which is, in its account of events up to 1915, a strikingly conventional nine-

11. Neilson, *How Diplomats Make War*, Introduction, pp. ix–x.

teenth-century fable of self-made success. Neilson tells us that
he first heard about Henry George from a Union Square soap-
box orator soon after he had come as a young immigrant of
eighteen to New York.[12] Born in 1867 in Birkenhead, Shropshire, England, Neilson (who used his mother's surname) was
the son of a "town's waiter," Francis Butters, and Isabella Neilson, who were both, at the time of their marriage, on the staff
of the Palatine Club in Liverpool. Through Mrs. Butters's aunt,
"one of the most famous cooks" in the vicinity, Neilson's parents "became acquainted with many of the 'grand' people about
the county," one of whom helped them to buy a restaurant
business in Liverpool, in which they prospered, rising to comfortable tradesman's status.[13] In religion Presbyterian, in political persuasion constitutional radicals, Neilson's parents seem
to have been stable citizens, devoted to family life, hard-work-
ing, pious, and self-respecting. Francis was sent to the industrial school of the Liverpool Institute and then apprenticed to
a firm of engineers. But he disliked the work, became restless,
and began to follow the players. He was shipped off to America, therefore, to make a new start for himself.

During his first hard years in New York—when he learned
about Henry George—Neilson alternated work as an extra
in the theater with manual labor and a program of reading
radical literature, history, and the classics in translation at the
public libraries. But soon his life began to follow the pattern
of other successful apprentice actors in the nineties. There was
a period of studying with Dion Boucicault, of acting with
William Gillette, of reviewing and writing plays, of lunching
with the musical crowd at Fleishman's. Neilson's social conscience was not neglected, however, for Georgism seems to
have been a popular faith among actors of the period.[14] Neilson
heard and read a good deal about the single tax, which fitted

12. Neilson, *My Life in Two Worlds*, I, 241.
13. *Ibid.*, p. 4.                    14. *Ibid.*, p. 241.

easily into the free-trade, anti-corn-law radicalism of his inherited family politics.

Having married an actress, Catherine Eva O'Gorman, Neilson took his wife back to England to live when he went in
1897 with Gillette's play *Secret Service* to London. There he
continued to enlarge his connections and to participate in various theatrical and musical enterprises until he became manager
of the Covent Garden Opera, a position which he held from
1900 to 1904. During these years in London he rubbed shoulders
with figures in the international world of the arts and met
English intellectuals, like Alfred Orage of the *New Age*. He
found that Georgism gained prestige as the program of Liberal
land reforms grew.

Neilson did not, however, cut himself off entirely from his
family in Liverpool and their social and political life. While
still at Covent Garden he stood as the Liberal candidate for
the Newport division of Shropshire (the Butters's county),
having been introduced to the Liberal committee by Edward
Hemmerde, a barrister of Liverpool.[15] The committee welcomed Neilson as a campaigner because he was a good speaker,
was well informed on questions pertaining to land taxation,
and knew the constituency. Although he was not elected to a
seat in Parliament until 1910, he continued to be a candidate
each year; after a quarrel with the Royal Opera Syndicate,
which ended his work as manager of Covent Garden, he became a full-time member of the Liberal party machine. He
spoke at by-elections all over England and acted as a liaison
man between the Liberals and Joseph Fels's League for the
Taxation of Land Values, which was pushing the party's program of agrarian reforms that materialized in the Land Bills
of 1909–10. Riding in on these successes, Neilson was finally
elected to Parliament in 1910, where he was, apparently, "in"
with the leading Liberals of his day, until he found himself a

15. *Ibid.*, p. 242.

member of the small, unpopular minority whose principles of Peace, Retrenchment, and Reform were discredited by the pressures of the war.

Traits of mentality and character which Neilson reveals in his autobiography are corroborated by his writings elsewhere and by various people who knew him.[16] He was openhearted, hotheaded, and credulous. By his own account, he often rushed into collaborations which ended without his having received whatever credit was due him, or he advocated policies for promoting the general good, with no other result to himself than quarrels and recriminations. Yet, his greatest talents lay in the managerial world of politics and the stage, where good looks,[17] charm, and hard work paid off. Intellectual though he was, with a diversity of cultural interests, his mind lacked depth and bite. But he was well read and well informed, thoroughly schooled in party dogma, and had that genuine respect for learning so often characteristic of self-made men. His political writing is not distinguished for style, nor is it well organized. His best plays and his novel, *A Strong Man's House*, had the knack of being timely and successful; read now, they want luster.

Neilson describes himself as lacking in push—justly, one feels, for, despite the fact that he had "succeeded," had made influential friends, had become a part of the public life of his day, and was frankly proud of having done all this, there was a careless, restless quality about him, and an underlying pas-

16. Neilson was born in 1867; he died on April 13, 1961, at the age of 94.

17. Photographs of Neilson in youth and middle age show "a fine head," rugged but regular features, a large, tall frame, and a good carriage. One contemporary remembers him, when he came to America in 1915, as a charming man and a careless dresser, who wore his hair in a shaggy mane and stuck little steel-rimmed glasses askew on his nose. Van Wyck Brooks remembers him as a *bon viveur*, B. W. Huebsch as courtly.

sivity. The person revealed in his reminiscences is never humorous or shrewd. The distressing and naïvely expressed resentment, self-justification, and suspicion which he showed in his later years must have been due in part to the fact that he by nature a simple man—unable to support the terrible moral and psychological burden that marriage to a rich woman imposed. The social disorientation, the leisure, the boredom, the importance, the presence of sycophants, the spending of somebody else's money would have their corroding effects on a more sinewy personality than his. But, whatever his limitations, he seems to have found a number of persons who genuinely liked him.

One associates Neilson's political activities with by-elections and debating halls, with the literalness and oratorical fervor of a reform propagandist, with the tensions in Parliament preceding the war. In contrast, the radicalism of Albert Jay Nock in 1915 lacked the color and action of Neilson's setting. As a fellow traveler with the American reformers and an editor on a muckraking magazine, Nock had led, in comparison to Neilson, a relatively unspectacular and undistinguished political life. Nor had he fully formulated the philosophy or had the experience as a writer by which he later made for himself a career as an intellectual historian and castigator of modern manners. A nonconformist by nature, he yet stood in line with the reformers of the prewar time, as his letters from this era prove. As he grew older, he cultivated a sense of history and of society which was closer to that of the aristocrat than to the practical idealism and progressivism of the muckrakers with whom he had associated.

Nock delighted in style and in mystification. Essentially a worldly man (for, under the dry moral scorn of the world, shows the man who intends to get on in it), he displayed a kind of fabulist's genius for giving his life distinction by making a legend out of himself.[18] This legend grew in his own mind, until he became, as he implies in the autobiography he wrote at the age of seventy, the archetype of the "superfluous man," rejecting and rejected by the materialism of American mass culture.

One aspect of Nock's legend-making faculty was a carefully nurtured reticence about his personal affairs. This characteristic, which contributed greatly to his reputation as an eccentric, manifested itself early in his life to his colleagues and even to his family, and it is one of the striking features of the *Memoirs of a Superfluous Man*, in which he has recorded so fully his intellectual history. Specific details about his life, especially his early career, have long been hard to come by, although there is sufficient information to outline his background, education, and professional training, as well as to describe his response to the *Zeitgeist*.[19]

The son of a clergyman, Albert Jay Nock was born into the polite world of an Episcopal rectory in a middle-class section

18. There is something about Nock's creation of a personal legend that suggests Constance Rourke's description of that peculiarly American faculty she finds in the frontier humorists. Indeed, there is something of the riverboat prestidigitator-in-narrative about Nock, though never the verbal exuberance. Francis Neilson's description in *The Story of "The Freeman"* of trying to pin Nock down to admitting what he knew and did not know and Nock's skillful elusiveness has an unintentionally humorous effect. A friend remembers how he sometimes liked to bemuse the inquisitor into his affairs by replying with "fantastic, confusing, soberly stated nonsense." See Francis J. Nock, ed., *Selected Letters of Albert Jay Nock*, p. 184.

19. For the information about Nock's life not supplied in his letters and his memoirs I am indebted to Francis J. Nock, his son; to Ruth Robinson and Catherine Wilson, his friends; and to his colleagues on the *Freeman*. The recent publication of a number of letters written during his association with the muckrakers has clarified the picture of his early sympathies and convictions, and Miss Robinson's "Memories of Albert Jay Nock," published with them, records a long association and some new facts.

of Brooklyn. He describes his descent as English and French.[20]
His paternal grandfather, a Staffordshire locksmith and a Dissenter, had come to America to superintend a steel mill. The
most interesting feature of his mother's heritage was her direct
descent from Chief Justice John Jay. Yet, Nock does not mention this fact in his autobiography, although it is said he took
much pride in the connection. He makes much, however, of
the Gallic skepticism to which he fancies he fell heir through
his mother's family, the French Jays. He attributes his sturdiness
of character and his feeling for language to his father's people,
and his interest in Greek and Latin to his father himself, who
was his first teacher. When Nock was ten years old, his family
moved to an isolated settlement on Lake Huron, where he was
educated entirely at home; six years later he was sent to a
frugal, Scotch Presbyterian boarding school in Illinois. He at-
tended college at an Episcopal institution, St. Stephen's (now
Bard) in New York State, and afterward, he says, "did grad-
uate work for the best part of three years in different institutions, shopping around irregularly like the . . . wandering
scholars of the middle ages." [21]

Nock does not record in his memoirs the fact that he was
ordained an Episcopal minister or that he performed parish
duties for a number of years before 1910. (Only in 1924 did
he apply for a deposition.) Nor does he tell us just how
and when he came to be a follower of Henry George or to be
associated with the muckrakers. He does say that he was
"emerging from the academic shades" just about the time of
George's second mayoralty campaign in New York and that
George seemed to him "a very great social philosopher who
had trained himself into a first-class polemicist, crusader, campaigner; a strange combination, the strangest imaginable." [22]

20. Albert Jay Nock, *Memoirs of a Superfluous Man,* pp. 7–14.
21. *Ibid.,* p. 97.                22. *Ibid.,* pp. 126–27.

Quoting Robert La Follette's remark that "George's social philosophy and his fiscal method, taken together, made a system 'against which nothing rational has ever been said or can be said,'" Nock expressed not only the "inevitable logic" of the single-tax philosophy which struck so many of his contemporaries but also the line which he consistently took in his writing on Georgism.[23] Yet, Nock added a twist characteristic of him in maintaining that the country was not ready for such fundamental reform. Admitting, then, that he was a single taxer, but saying that the single tax was not practicable, Nock joined up with some of George's disciples—Louis F. Post, C. B. Fillebrown, George Record, Newton Baker, Brand Whitlock, William Jay Gaynor, and Herbert Quick—and with the muckrakers on the *American Magazine*, where he was a member of the editorial board from 1910 to 1915.

Lincoln Steffens, describing this board, speaks of John Phillips, Ida Tarbell, Newton Baker, Finley Peter Dunne, and "that finished scholar, Albert Jay Nock," who later came "to put in mastered [*sic*] English for [the *American Magazine*] the editorials which expressed with his grave smile and chuckling tolerance 'our' interpretations of things human." The muckrakers, whose main business was reform, were "to edit a writer's magazine." [24]

The psychological and aesthetic distance which, Steffens's remark implies, Nock put between himself and the reformers of the early 1900s, he seems always to have established, in one form or another, between himself and the world. Versions of the Nock manner and aloofness come from other contemporaries of this and of the *Freeman* period. For some he was an admirable aristocrat of the spirit; for others, disingenuous and a snob. Perverse, eccentric, talented—that was Nock's "character" in the twenties, and, in an age in which idiosyncrasy could still be regarded with nineteenth-century indulgence, his passion

23. *Ibid.*, p. 127.          24. Steffens, *Autobiography*, II, 536.

for secrecy, his sudden withdrawals, and his playing of roles became part of the folklore of the time. The quirks of his personality were more often regarded as tonic than as repellent or absurd. All in all, Nock was capable of inspiring strong aversions and also, particularly among women, strong loyalties.

Representations of the later—what we might call the final—Albert Jay Nock have the effect of obstructing the attempt to see him as he was in the days of the muckrakers. There is the Nock whom Russell Kirk chose to occupy an honorable place in the conservative tradition of Burke and John Adams,[25] and who has become a guiding figure for the new libertarian conservatives. There is the Nock who baited Roosevelt and fulminated against the fuzzy-headed New Dealers in his letters to his wealthy Philadelphia patrons, Mrs. Edmund Cadwallader Evans and Miss Ellen Winsor, and to other friends. There is the Nock who, in the forties, in certain of his articles in the *Atlantic* laid himself open to charges of anti-Semitism.[26] There is the superfluous man, already mentioned, whose urbane, highly intellectualized and somewhat pretentious *Memoirs* traced a growing alienation from American life with *The Education of Henry Adams* as a model.[27] (The irony seems flat, the experience meager, beside the great original.) Although the Nock of the muckraking days and of the *Freeman* made a principle of open-mindedness which withered with the years, one finds qualities that remained throughout his mature life: the same intensity, the same lack of spontaneity, the same striking talent enforced by a canny ability to get on, the same arrogance, and

25. Kirk, *The Conservative Mind*, pp. 420–21. Kirk recognizes also Nock's Jeffersonianism but finds him, nonetheless, strongly conservative.

26. See "The Jewish Problem in America," *The Atlantic Monthly*, CLXVII (June, 1941), 699–706, and CLXVIII (July, 1941), 67–76.

27. Nock, in Garrison, ed., *Letters from Albert Jay Nock*, pp. 129–30; 178. The book, published in 1943, was indeed acclaimed on the jacket by Henrick Wilhelm Van Loon as a second *Education of Henry Adams*, bidding "fair to become one of the most important documents of our era of despair."

the same features of a literary personality which combined self-satisfaction, principles tenaciously held, polish and clarity of expression, an intellection sometimes specious and sometimes telling—the whole wanting in flashes of life-giving insight.

Such was the background and character of the two men whom Brand Whitlock brought together in 1915. Neilson's affiliation with the Liberals was shattered; his political career would soon terminate altogether. Nock, as a roving journalist, was ready for anything. Both were without independent incomes and expected to live by their wits. Could not the Englishman's range of political knowledge, his experience and prestige be helpful to an enterprising American journalist? Could not this journalist with his energy and drive assist Neilson in establishing himself in the literary world of America, to which he was turning his thoughts? Besides, there was the message of *How Diplomats Make War*, which must be sure to find an audience.

When, in the autumn of 1915, Neilson finally came to America, bringing his wife and two daughters, Nock was instrumental in helping him to arrange for quarters and to explore the possibilities for making a living. The manuscript of *How Diplomats Make War* had been left, at Neilson's suggestion, with the publisher B. W. Huebsch, who had given no definite answer as to its future. Now Nock and Neilson went to see him, with the result that he agreed to bring the book out anonymously (with the signature "By a British Statesman").[28] Nock appended his own name to the introduction, from which I have quoted. The book caused a gratifying stir. The following winter Neilson was engaged by a syndicate to lecture in various cities across the country on the imperialist causes of the war.

During his stay in Chicago he was entertained by Helen

28. Neilson, *The Story of "The Freeman,"* p. 8.

Swift Morris, the daughter of Gustavus Swift (who had
founded Swift and Company) and the widow of Edward
Morris (whose father, Nelson, had also been one of the first
great packers in the city).[29] Neilson had been introduced to
the Edward Morrises in London in 1912, when they were the
guests of honor at a dinner given by Lloyd George and Sir
Henry Dalziel at the House of Commons. A friendship had
arisen and was renewed whenever the Morrises were in England. This latest reunion with Helen Swift Morris in Chicago
was to change the course of Neilson's life.

He was divorced from his first wife in the spring of 1917.
Mrs. Morris proposed to him that summer, and they were immediately married—to the great amazement of Chicago society, Neilson says, and to the dismay of her children. Neilson
was fifty years old. He had been an actor, a playwright, a radical politician. For all his standing among the Liberal parlia-
mentarians, he was now an exile and an impecunious free
lance. Mrs. Morris was middle-aged also, and the mother of four
grown sons and daughters. A strong hostility toward Neilson
immediately arose in the young Morrises and among the Swift
relatives, a hostility which continued to be the source of much
pain on all sides throughout Helen Neilson's lifetime. At best,
Neilson was scorned as a high-brow intruder into a heavy,
conventional, plutocratic world; at worst, the accusations of
fortune-hunting thundered. Neilson himself, in self-justification,
makes much of the fact that his union with Helen Swift gave
her a chance to be what she had wanted to be ever since her
college days at Wellesley, a high-brow.[30] Indeed, for the
twenty-eight years of this extraordinary marriage, which

29. Three packing firms, Armour, Swift, and Morris, planned in 1902
to consolidate into one firm, the National Packing Company, but "public
opinion was against it," writes Louis F. Swift, the son of Gustavus, in a
biography of his father, *The Yankee of the Yards*, written in collaboration with Arthur Van Vlissingen, Jr., p. 209.

30. Neilson, *My Life in Two Worlds*, II, 21–34.

Neilson frankly describes as passionless and which was marred by Mrs. Neilson's long, neurotic illness and much unhappiness on Neilson's side, their intellectual companionship and their magnificent philanthropic gestures toward the intellectual life, which his social experience and outlook suggested, seem to have been the absorbing, pleasurable part of their life together.

"Thrifty, sluggish, bourgeois, with a gloomy vein of Teutonic pessimism, the Swifts have added little to the social gaiety of Chicago," wrote Dixon Wecter of the family into which Neilson had married.[31] Mrs. Neilson herself is said to have been a serious and responsible woman, completely in control of the financial intricacies of her empire. Following a familiar pattern of graduates from the Eastern colleges who return to their home towns, she had found an outlet for her intellectual bent in social service and had worked for many years with Jenkin Lloyd Jones, the famous Unitarian reformer. She was, as a member of the *Freeman* staff remembers, "as liberal as such a rich woman can be." [32] She had belonged to a Browning club and, with her first husband, had decorated the library of their mansion on Drexel Boulevard with "some fine examples of the Barbizon school," [33] like other millionaires in Chicago. But Francis Neilson's wider aesthetic tastes and his extensive knowledge of political theory opened up many new avenues for patronage of the arts and gave background to her humanitarian activities. The change, however, by no means let in the atmosphere of an artistic Bohemia. The Neilsons were inclined toward the grand manner: a hundred people came of an evening, for example, to hear the husband read a paper, carefully annotated by his wife, on *The Ring and the Book*, while dinners for distinguished businessmen, like Sir Thomas Lipton, al-

31. Wecter, *The Saga of American Society*, p. 147.
32. From an interview with B. W. Huebsch, spring, 1953.
33. Neilson, *My Life in Two Worlds*, II, 26.

ternated with dinners for distinguished scholars and guests of the University of Chicago. As an outlet for his political energies, Neilson decided to work with John Haynes Holmes as co-editor of *Unity*, a biweekly magazine of a reformist cast, which Mrs. Neilson helped to support and which was sponsored by the Unitarian church.

The intellectual venture that was to be the most significant and the most notable philanthropical enterprise of the Neilsons' lives, the founding of the *Freeman*, was several years in the making and arose out of the fact that Neilson had, after his marriage, remained in touch with Albert Jay Nock, whose connection with the *American Magazine* had ended after 1915. A frequent visitor at the mansion on Drexel Boulevard and at Mrs. Neilson's summer home in Green Lake, Wisconsin, Nock often discussed politics with the Neilsons. They talked in the context of the two men's shared convictions: of the dangers of "latter-day liberalism" and its betrayal of the fundamental principles of freedom during the war, of the threats to individual liberty of "the nostrums of Socialism and bureaucratic paternalism," of the evolution of the state, of Georgism.[34] The sense that a great tradition might be lost seems to have been very strong in these conversations; the tone was, doubtless, in-

34. Neilson's record of these talks and their first fruits appears in *The Story of "The Freeman,"* pp. 25, 15; and in *My Life in Two Worlds*, II, 40. Villard, in his account of the reorganization of the *Nation* in 1918, does not speak of the offer to buy the magazine, nor of the financial arrangement about Nock, although he expresses pleasure at securing so able an editor as he. See Villard, *Fighting Years*, pp. 49–50. Villard mentions also the generous financial support of Mr. and Mrs. Francis Neilson for the publication of a fortnightly supplement on international relations which began to appear in October, 1918. A letter from Nock to Neilson, dated November 14, 1919, discusses a proposal made to both men by Villard that Nock return to the *Nation*. Nock declines, saying that he has come to consider the magazine wrongheaded; and he suggests that Neilson withdraw any support. See Francis J. Nock, ed., *Selected Letters of Albert Jay Nock*, pp. 95–96.

tensified by the tensions of the times. The idea of reviving an important political heritage by giving their views public expression arose, for there was no powerful organ existing which did so. Neilson claims that at this point and at Nock's suggestion, they played with the thought of buying the *Nation* for their purpose. Villard, when approached, scouted the proposal but evinced enough interest in their economic and anti-state theories to be willing to give them an outlet on the paper. It was arranged, Neilson says, that Nock should join the staff on the basis of a subsidy from Mrs. Neilson. (Nock's name appears on the masthead as associate editor from July, 1918, to December, 1919; he wrote special articles and also unsigned editorials on various subjects.) In the fall of 1919 came the idea of starting a completely new journal, the initiation of which Neilson attributes entirely to his wife and to Nock.

In the autumn of 1919 Helen told me that she had heard from Nock and that he wished to come to the farm to see us. I little dreamed it was to be a momentous visit. Each day I went out bass fishing, as the season was at its height. In my absence Helen introduced Nock to what she called "woodsing," her favorite recreation in the country—that of gathering wild orchids and other rare plants for her wildflower garden. I could not picture Albert enjoying the horticultural delights Helen loved so much.

After he had been with us for a week, one night at the dinner table Helen said, "We have a surprise for you. We're going to start a paper of our own."

The first idea was to be a weekly and I should be the editor, free to come and go, and Nock would be the "chore man," to use his own expression. I am afraid I put a damper on their ardor by asking many questions they had not considered. How was I to be editor of a paper and to go to Europe year after year as Helen desired? She wanted me to show her the Continent, as I knew it.

Another difficulty was that of finding a staff competent to undertake such an enterprise. I presumed that the weeklies then being published had the best people obtainable for the work. Although these questions posed difficulties, both Helen and Nock insisted that the attempt was worth making. He returned to New York determined to see what could be done.[35]

The passage above appears in Neilson's autobiography (containing a fairly restrained version of Nock's relation to the *Freeman*). It is colored by the context in which it was first written: *The Story of "The Freeman,"* a pamphlet which Neilson composed and issued in 1946, the year after Nock's death. Anyone familiar with this document, which aroused strong partisanship in old *Freeman* circles, must be struck by the bitter frankness with which Neilson accuses Nock of exploiting both Mrs. Neilson for her money and himself for his knowledge during the period that led to the founding of the magazine. Written long after the event and discharging a resentment against Nock which had been greatly inflamed by the course of their joint editorship of the *Freeman* and then, seemingly, stored up for years, Neilson's charges against Nock are arresting but must be weighed against Neilson's anger, especially when he attacks Nock's sciolism.[36] Viewed in the light of his outrage, Neilson's disclaimer of any part in the inception of the paper and of any initial interest in it is suspect. Certainly his commitment to the political position it would express was strong; he had played a substantial part in putting the paper into operation; one cannot believe that Mrs. Neilson's gift to her husband was entirely unsought or unwelcome.[37] But, however tendentious Neilson's memories, one can believe that Nock's activity

35. Neilson, *My Life in Two Worlds*, II, 41; see also *The Story of "The Freeman,"* pp. 19–20.

36. Neilson, *The Story of "The Freeman,"* pp. 14–19.

37. It is said that Neilson regretted printing *The Story of "The Freeman."* The self-revelation was as damaging to him as his accusations were to Nock, The latter, unfortunately, has provided no check on Neilson's account; the description of the *Freeman* in *Memoirs of a Superfluous Man* begins with the publication of the magazine in 1920 and does not mention persons by name.

was a very strong factor in the origin of the paper. If his motive of self-interest was powerful and his use of the Neilsons skillful (as seems quite likely), one cannot but admire the quality of his imagination. Nock fits well into this atmosphere, where money gave power to realize grand ideas and to ratify social consciences. What more useful executor could Mrs. Neilson have found than this reformer and moralist, this worldly, cultivated, practical scholar-gentleman, this ambitious talented journalist, whose sense of opportunity and place was so strong, who could visualize a daring plan, calculate the risks, and summon the energy to put it through? Neilson seems the more ingenuous figure in this American success story, and he is the richer by far, but Nock is clearly the abler.

Once initiated, the plan for a new magazine materialized very quickly. The Neilsons spent the winter of 1919–20 in New York at the Ritz Carlton, where they conferred with Nock almost daily. By spring the magazine was organized and the staff assembled.

The conception had from the very first been a large one: to found a paper of quality and scope, at least comparable to and, if possible, excelling the best established weeklies of the period. Because of Francis Neilson's English background and his experience in Liberal politics, the magazine was to be international in scope and, it was hoped, to have an international as well as a national circulation. Although the primary interest was to be political, the paper was also to concern itself, like its models, the English weeklies, with criticism of the arts and with the publication of creative literature. In all fields it expected to maintain a high quality of writing and to draw upon European as well as American contributors.

Mrs. Neilson had offered to subsidize the magazine completely for three trial years. Neilson says that his wife "set her face against taking paid advertisements"; their absence was advanced as setting a high tone and keeping the paper free of commercial restraints.[38] B. W. Huebsch, the publisher, recalls, on the other hand, that "the subject never arose" until he introduced it, only to demonstrate that "none of the journals of opinion ever commanded enough advertising to make any difference" and that "it would cost us more to maintain a department and alienate the necessary space than we could possibly get for it." [39] The name for the new publication, chosen after some discussion among the editors and Huebsch, was the one proposed by Neilson, *The Freeman*, "because [he] wished it implied in the title that the editorial policy was based upon a theory of economic emancipation." [40]

One indication of the magnitude of the founders' intentions is that there was no question but that their magazine, backed though it was by a Chicago fortune, should be published in New York and not in Chicago. For New York in 1920, as never before, was the inevitable city in which to publish a national weekly with an international outlook and to find writing talent to draw on for editors and contributors. A few years earlier, during the "Chicago renaissance," the choice might not have been so easy, but the intellectual prestige of this Middle Western city had greatly declined during and after the war, although Chicago still symbolized for some critics the force of a native culture in contrast to the decadence of the genteel East. H. L. Mencken, for example, explaining American culture to the readers of the London *Nation* in 1920, could write that New York had "ceased long ago to hold any leadership in that department of the national life of the republic which has to do

---

38. Neilson, *The Story of "The Freeman,"* p. 48.
39. From a letter to the author, June 19, 1961.
40. Neilson, *The Story of "The Freeman,"* p. 25. In two letters written by Nock to Neilson other names—"Common Sense," "The Pathfinder"—and the possibility of finding something new by translating foreign titles are discussed. See Francis J. Nock, ed., *Selected Letters of Albert Jay Nock*, p. 94.

with beautiful letters," and that nearly every writer who is "indubitably an American in every pulse-beat, snort and adenoid . . . has some sort of connection with the Gargantuan and inordinate abattoir by Lake Michigan." [41] This opinion is expressive of that impulse to discover an indigenous literature that had made Chicago for a brief time an avant-garde city for such critics, writers of fiction, and poets as Floyd Dell, Carl Sandburg, Francis Hackett, Edgar Lee Masters, Robert Morss Lovett, Ben Hecht, and Sherwood Anderson. However, the East had always exerted a strong pull, and by 1920 many of these writers had long since moved to New York—for example, Dell to edit the *Masses,* Hackett to join the *New Republic*, and Sherwood Anderson to seek intellectual companionship. *Poetry* was still published in Chicago, but the fortnightly *Dial,* of which the city had been so proud, had been moved to New York in 1918, two years before its conversion into a purely literary monthly.[42]

The Chicago awakening had, after all, been part of a larger phase of national renaissance, an effort to re-evaluate American life and its tradition. It had its counterpart on the East coast, announced by Van Wyck Brooks's *America's Coming-of-Age.* The war had interrupted, then restimulated and redirected the process by giving America a greater consciousness of Europe,

41. Mencken, "The Literary Capital of the United States." American Literary Supplement to *The Nation* (London), XXVII (April 17, 1920), 91–92.

42. Harold Stearns, writing of his work on the *Dial* during the six months before it was moved to New York, describes its place in Chicago culture: "When I went there, although very few people read it, Chicagoans were still inordinately proud of the *Dial.* It was almost like a civic accomplishment, a living refutation to the Eastern ill-wishers who said that Chicago cared only about meat-packing and making money. I was astonished at the number of people I met in Chicago who seldom—if ever—looked at the magazine, but who could nevertheless tell you its history and string off the names of some of its early famous contributors." (From *The Street I Know,* pp. 154–55.)

so that the perspective in 1920 was both national and international. Van Wyck Brooks comes nearer than Mencken to expressing the tone and rationale of American cultural criticism in 1920 when, accepting the centralization of the literary life in New York as a fact, he finds it a cause for congratulation:

It is not vitality that makes a literary center, but the presence of intellectual world currents and the peculiar intellectual intensity they give birth to. Perhaps we may say that the advantage of New York as a literary center lies precisely in the fact that *it is* [sic] the "least American" of cities, the most exposed, that is, to the perpetual contagion of Europe.[43]

In magazines and publishing, the changes which had begun to take place in New York during the last decade had produced a situation highly favorable to a new venture in periodical criticism such as the *Freeman.* Out of the ashes of the muckraking magazines, the genteel literary monthlies, and the short-lived attempts at cultural criticism, such as the *Seven Arts,* was arising a vigorous new intellectual leadership in politics and the arts. The *Nation,* under Villard and the literary editorship of Carl Van Doren, and the *New Republic,* under Herbert Croly and Francis Hackett, were liberal journals of much distinction. The new *Dial* was beginning to assume a strong position as an arbiter of the creative arts. These magazines, together with Mencken's *Smart Set,* Frank Crowninshield's *Vanity Fair,* and the leftist *Liberator,* under Floyd Dell and Max Eastman, employed many advanced writers of the prewar period and were attracting to jobs in editing and reviewing the young intellectuals from the Eastern colleges and those who had just returned from the war. There was everywhere an effort to search out new talent among Americans and to keep the lines open for European contributors. Parallel to the activity of the magazines was that of the experimental publishing houses,

43. "A Reviewer's Notebook," *The Freeman,* II (Dec. 1, 1920), 287.

B. W. Huebsch, Inc., Boni and Liveright, Harcourt, Brace and Howe.

The selection of the staff of the *Freeman* represented a half-daring, half-orthodox use of some of the best professional and amateur talent New York had to offer. With his years of experience in reform journalism and a recent stint on the *Nation* behind him, Albert Jay Nock undoubtedly had a far more intimate knowledge of the whole literary situation than did Francis Neilson. The latter, while attributing the choice of a name and the formulation of the editorial policy of the *Freeman* to himself, says that the matter of personnel was left entirely up to Nock. Yet, other evidence shows a less clear division of labor in the matter of organizing the staff and a fuller picture of the influences which gave form and texture to the enterprise.

B. W. Huebsch, who was the publisher of the magazine and president of The Freeman Corporation, says he took on the paper through Neilson. (The two had met in London before the war;[44] a further connection had been established between Huebsch and Neilson over the publication of *How Diplomats Make War*.) Described by Hart Crane in 1920 as the most cultivated publisher in America, Huebsch had for the past decade given aid and comfort to avant-garde writers by printing such books as James Joyce's *The Portrait of the Artist as a Young Man* and the early criticism of Van Wyck Brooks, *America's Coming-of-Age* and *Letters and Leadership*. A liberal in politics as well as in publishing, Huebsch says that he had a commitment to the single tax which he came to from his good friendship with Joseph Fels. With his professional knowledge of publishing and his connections with the New York literati, Huebsch provided splendid assistance in the whole process of setting up the *Freeman*. And he helped to keep it going: dur-

44. From an interview with the author, spring, 1952.

ing the four years of its life he worked as both manager and contributor in close cooperation with the editors.

It was Huebsch who assured the *Freeman* a place in the front lines when he wrote to Van Wyck Brooks, then living in California, to ask him to join the magazine as literary editor. Brooks, at that time thirty-three years old, was at work on *The Ordeal of Mark Twain.* With the precocious *Wine of the Puritans* and his two "leadership" books behind him, he had become a key figure in the avant-garde of American criticism. If his reputation was limited to a select group, his standing among them was very high—as an editor of the *Seven Arts* and the fortnightly *Dial,* as a lieutenant of Randolph Bourne, and as a prophet of literary radicalism. "There had been no time for many years, it seems, during which Van Wyck Brooks had not been straining to read the face of the United States," [45] wrote Paul Rosenfeld in 1924 of the *Seven Arts* days. He continues rhapsodically to describe the impression Brooks made in the editorial office of this magazine:

When finally Brooks himself with his simple Harvard blandness, his smile like a pleased savage's, his cockscomb of hair, his abrupt pumping handshake and his watch chain depending from the lapel of his miraculously precise and well-pressed coat, walked into the office of the infant magazine and joined in the conversation, he brought in the guise of his solid knowledge of the American background, his long-refined ideas, his piercing insight into the national temper, some of the fattest kernels poured for the common good into that busily grinding mill. With him came the philosophical and intellectual basis of the movement, the analytical scheme of the past.[46]

Brooks struck many others in the literary world of the early twenties as the avatar of the creative life: when he came to the *Freeman,* one of the editorial assistants remembers that it seemed as if "all the young writers in New York tramped up

45. Rosenfeld, *Port of New York,* p. 19.        46. *Ibid.,* p. 48.

and down the steps to his office all day long." As the leader of
the literary radicals, Brooks was the most distinguished addition to the staff made by the founding editors, and the most
experienced writer. Operating somewhat independently of the
regular routine of the editorial office, he came in only two days
a week and was a law unto himself.

Nock, the wheelhorse of the whole enterprise, was responsible for the other appointments. One of these was Suzanne
La Follette, a young relative of the Senator from Wisconsin
and a philosophical anarchist—not a single taxer—whom Nock
had brought from the *Nation*. (A letter from Nock, written
at the time to Francis Neilson, takes up the question of Miss
La Follette's wages as "troublesome": he wants to keep ex-
penses down, but Miss La Follette is getting $45 at the *Nation*
and to offer her $50 seems only decent. Besides it's a matter of
" 'getting our pages' properly filled.") [47] Nock also found
Walter G. Fuller, an Englishman, who is remembered as a
"splendid rewrite man" and the author of witty tales for articles
and reviews in the *Freeman*. To fill the other place on the editorial staff, Nock appointed Geroid Tanquary Robinson, who
later became Director of Columbia University's Russian Institute.[48] Robinson, a young Virginian, had been educated at Stan-
ford and Columbia, where at the time of his appointment to the
*Freeman*, he was a lecturer in modern European history. He
was a veteran of the American air service and a former editor
of the fortnightly *Dial*.

Besides the editors there were at the *Freeman* office two recent graduates from women's colleges to do secretarial work
and to take charge of making up the paper: Lucy Taussig, who

47. Francis J. Nock, ed., *Selected Letters of Albert Jay Nock*, p.
97.

48. B. W. Huebsch says that two people presented themselves for this
appointment, Robinson and Lewis Mumford. (From a letter to the author, Dec. 27, 1961).

came from Wellesley and was the niece of the famous econo-
mist at Harvard, and Emilie McMillan, from Smith.

Although the names of Francis Neilson, Albert Jay Nock,
and B. W. Huebsch appeared on the masthead for the first two
months, the members of the editorial staff were with the *Freeman* from the first, and, with the exception of Walter Fuller,
who returned to England in 1922, they remained on the paper
for its lifetime.

Differences of opinion as well as of experience existed among
the members of the editorial board. The strongly individualistic, single-tax line of the two chief editors was not sympathetic to Brooks, who was a socialist, while his championship of
"the new writers," as he tells us, ran counter to the literary
preferences of Albert Jay Nock, who took these same writers
to task for failing to follow nineteenth-century rules of
decorum.[49] Yet, conflicts in conviction and taste such as these
did not destroy the cohesiveness of the *Freeman*. The principle
of unity was of that subtle, dialectical kind that can mold a
magazine and give it a definable character. To define it is to
describe the history and content of the *Freeman;* suffice it to
say here that the relatively free, open, and changing milieu of
1920 gave the magazine a good start and was partly responsible for holding it together. So also was the standard of free
expression of opinion under which the editorial board operated.
Nock's description of its functioning is borne out by the people
who worked with him; it constituted for them one of the
distinctive features of their association with the magazine:

I never gave any directions or orders; sometimes a suggestion but
only as the other staff-members made suggestions, provisionally,
and under correction from anyone who had anything better to

49. Brooks says in *Days of the Phoenix* that Nock was "scarcely aware
of the so-called literary renaissance of which the *Freeman* was obviously
one of the symbols. . . ." (p. 59).

offer. I did not assign subjects for editorial treatment. Each of us picked his own, and we discussed them together once a week.[50]

In other words there seems to have been a genuine respect for reasoned opinion as such on the *Freeman*. This feeling, heightened doubtless by a revulsion from the hysteria and thought control of the war years and their aftermath, was a marked characteristic of the intellectual life of the early twenties. To make a special kind of editorial strength out of it, as Nock did, was one evidence of his brilliance as a journalist.

Some of the first contributors must have been secured during the winter as part of the process of organizing the *Freeman*. The list includes English and American writers, nearly all of whom were in professional journalism, politics, or the university world; many of them were contributing to other British and American weeklies. Amos Pinchot, Louis Levine, Lewis Mumford, and F. W. Garrison (an expositor of the single tax) wrote short editorials; longer articles on political and cultural subjects came from G. D. H. Cole, J. D. Beresford, Laurence Housman, and Gilbert Cannan in England, and from Mumford, Arthur Gleason, R. G. Lowie, John S. Codman, and William C. Bullitt at home. Ernest Boyd, Howard Mumford Jones, Louis Untermeyer, and Percy Boynton wrote about literature, and Walter Prichard Eaton about the theater.

Offices for the editorial staff were taken at 32 West 58th Street but were soon moved downtown to 116 West 13th Street. Although Huebsch acted in the capacity of manager of the *Freeman*, he turned over the actual finances to an expert accountant from the Swift firm, who was responsible for the $70,000 a year (more or less) which Mrs. Neilson provided for running expenses. Charles B. Falls was asked to design the distinctive type for the heading, and a small flurry occurred when it was discovered that a Negro newspaper in Indiana had

50. Albert Jay Nock, *Memoirs of a Superfluous Man*, p. 169.

been for several years calling itself the *Freeman*.[51] But its owners were persuaded by an emissary from Mrs. Neilson to sell their right to the name. On February 18, 1920, an announcement of the new weekly appeared in the newspapers and journals throughout the country (see Appendix).

The *Freeman* was modeled, as Nock has said, "in format and general appearance after the style of the London Spectator," and this plan was adhered to throughout the four years of publication.[52] Similar to the *Spectator* in its arrangement of material, the American magazine was divided topically into the following sections:

Current Comment: single paragraphs or groups of paragraphs on the issues of the week; unsigned, but written by members of the editorial staff.

Topics of the Day: editorials of a page or more in length, treating a variety of topics in economics, politics, cultural criticism; unsigned, but written by members of the staff, with occasional contributions from other writers.

The Middle Articles: longer articles, less specific in character than the topics, treating a wide range of social and artistic subjects; signed by a wide range of contributors.

Letters to the Editors: usually two pages in all, many letters short essays in themselves, either informative or polemical, on many subjects of current interest.

Miscellany: a collection of short paragraphs or essays, usually light or reminiscent in tone, serving as a kind of index to the manners and mores of the period; signed Journeyman, they were written by various members of the staff and by certain steady contributors.

Books: usually three or four full-length reviews of a page or

---

51. This was also the name of a paper established by Walt Whitman in Brooklyn in 1849. Van Wyck Brooks called this fact to the attention of the *Freeman's* readers in an early issue of the magazine.

52. Albert Jay Nock, *Memoirs of a Superfluous Man*, p. 167.

page and a half (signed); a group of one-paragraph comments under the title "Shorter Notices" (unsigned); and "The Reviewer's Notebook," the trademark of Van Wyck Brooks, either an essay in literary criticism or a review. The Notebook always was the last item in the magazine.

These staple divisions were interspersed in each issue with one or more additional departments: Theatre, Music, Art, and Letters from Abroad. There were always some works of the "creative imagination"—poems, vignettes, chapters from forthcoming books, biographies, notebooks, memoirs, occasionally a short story.

The total effect of the periodical—with its English spelling, its two-column quarto pages, usually running to the number of twenty-four, its precise, clear type,[53] its good quality of paper— was one of substance, of traditional nineteenth-century elegance. This solid, well-bred appearance was achieved to a certain degree by the *Freeman's* liberal contemporaries, but it stood in marked contrast to the leftist *Liberator*, with its cartoons and tabloid look, and the aesthetic *Dial*, whose pages of a single column in large type, reproductions of modern art, and pervasive color, light, and space were airily distinguished and modern.

The reasons for the editors' choice of a strictly English model for an American magazine have not been recorded. It was, after all, founded to express the views of an Englishman. One suspects, however, some measure of calculated idiosyncrasy—some intention to enhance the individualism of the paper as a whole. But, if there was a certain preciousness in its imitation of an English format and in its English orthography, the majority of the readers of the new magazine took this in

53. Three sizes of type were used: standard for the long editorials, middle articles, and lead book reviews, and "The Reviewer's Notebook;" a smaller type for all other material, except quotations and letters to the editor, which were all in fine print.

good part as a commendable expression of spirit; or, if they were conscious of the claims of an American language, they were more impressed by the wit and intellectual soundness of the material. For example, this excerpt from a letter to the editors in an early issue:

Sirs: I like most things about your first issue so much that I fear I shall weakly continue my subscription even tho you are counter-revolutionary in your spelling. But how can anyone in Noah Webster's America put any genuin [*sic*] feeling into an appeal to heed the claims of the "Labour" movement. . . . It is, if you like, a pin-prick; but it is one which you might spare many of your readers, I should think, without much danger of offending any. For surely few of the small and select group of Anglo-file "our-ists" will read the *Freeman*, even if bribed by the tempting bait of "Labour." [54]

The back page of the magazine was always given over to messages to subscribers and potential subscribers. Written by B. W. Huebsch, these messages were urbane, sometimes witty, informative descriptions of the virtues of the radical criticism to which the *Freeman* was dedicated. In keeping with the whole tone of the magazine, Huebsch wrote with the courteous assumption that the American reading public was literate, disinterested, and eager for enlightenment. With this assumption about its audience, the *Freeman* began, as Charles Beard put it, to scatter "acid on many a sacred convention." [55] The intellectual forces which Mrs. Neilson's sponsorship had marshaled were ready to proceed along their highly distinctive way.

54. "Letters to the Editors," *The Freeman*, I (March 31, 1920), 58.
55. Quoted in Albert Jay Nock, *Memoirs of a Superfluous Man*, p. 171.

# Chapter Two
# A Radical Magazine

In 1920, a year frequently described as pivotal in American cultural history, so much was going on in the way of questioning, revolt, and assimilation of the new in manners, morals, and the arts that the serious social-mindedness which expressed itself in politics has often been minimized by interpreters of the intellectual life of the period. *Main Street*, "the first genuinely popular novel to embody the moral revolt against convention," [1] and *This Side of Paradise*, as a harbinger of the Jazz Age, are traditionally cited to signify the tone of the new decade. Or 1920 has been described as the time when "the political strain" inherited from Shaw and Wells, hung in the balance with the aesthetic, only to give way.[2] But, in fact, a politico-economic, broadly social interest was a significant, vital feature of American opinion for the first years of the period. During this time the currents of prewar political and literary radicalism, so weakened by the war period itself, were revivified by what followed: the powerful labor movements in all countries of the Western world, the moral and economic questions concerning the peace, and the establishment of the Soviet State. In politics many of the prewar ideas of socialism, anarchism, and liberalism were being reviewed, as was the whole question of sovereignty. Syndicalism, guild socialism, direct action were in the air as forms of industrialism, and the land issue was not entirely forgotten, constituting part of the platform of a third-party group of progressives, the Committee of Forty-Eight.[3] The emergence of Marxism as a powerful

1. Cowley, ed., *After the Genteel Tradition*, p. 242.
2. Mizener, *The Far Side of Paradise*, p. 112.
3. This committee united with the American Labor Party, founded in

ideology in America had just begun. In literary criticism the theme of the writer and worker, explored by the middle-class radicals of the previous decade, could in this atmosphere still carry weight. All in all, there was not only an animated re-examination of various kinds of political and economic belief but a hopeful open-mindedness toward new theories and new techniques.

To discuss the characteristic freedom of the twenties only in the context of revolt from convention, of personal liberation, is, then, a distortion of the spirit of the first years of the decade; for the association of freedom with knowledge, rightly used for social progress, and with the social as well as the individual conscience is so strong that one almost inevitably thinks of enlightenment in the classic, eighteenth-century sense. The most ambitious social critique of the period, *Civilization in the United States* (1922), professed to be written in the spirit of the Encyclopedists.[4] If *This Side of Paradise* was a representa-tive book of 1920, so also was *The Economic Consequences of the Peace.* And both caught on. Keynes's book appealed to its readers not only because it expressed, with the authority of charts and graphs, disillusionment with the peace but also be-cause its implication was that the right use of economic knowl-edge could set the world in order again. This climate of opinion is what the *Freeman* implied in its prospectus when it spoke of "the new sense of inquiry and the new sense of responsibility which recent events [had] liberated."

A feeling of despair about American society was undoubt-edly very strong. Frederick Hoffman, in his book on the twenties, links the wholesale denigration of American in-stitutions in *Civilization in the United States* to the fact that

---

1919, to form the Farmer-Labor Party, which, in 1920, polled 300,000 votes. The Socialists refused to join and nominated Debs on their own ticket.

4. Stearns, ed., *Civilization in the United States*, p. iv.

the hopes for a better world which had inspired "the moral, intellectual, and aesthetic resurgence" of 1915 were "all but abandoned by the end of World War I." [5] Yet, this interpretation is brought into question by the liberal periodical literature of the years which followed, through 1921 at least, for this literature conveys an inescapably strong impression of the belief in and commitment to social progress just described. Although belief had to struggle with postwar cynicism and personal hopelessness, it either derived from the conflict a kind of strength, or, being overcome, at least kept the individual looking outwards.

It was into this atmosphere that the editors of the *Freeman* introduced, with a decidedly successful effect as far as the intelligentsia were concerned, their radical paper. That this radicalism was not a political staple, like that of the *Liberator*, but rather a philosophical anarchist's conception of progress to be effected by nonpolitical means was not at first understood by the *Freeman's* public. Nor was the fact that its editorial policy was formed as a conscious attack on political liberalism. With such a policy the paper stood apart from dominant forces on the left. Emanating from a theory of agrarian reform which had not been entirely eclipsed by the war and from a theory of the state which was associated with the whole important body of thought that had arisen since 1900 to explore the origin and nature of sovereignty, the *Freeman's* political editorials were unique in American journalism. But, different as its opinion was from other kinds of advanced politics in the period, the magazine was capable of serving as a focal point for liberal-leftist issues in 1920. Hostile to American socialism, the *Freeman* was open-minded about those forms of industrial organization that would circumvent state control, about syndicalism, direct action, and guild socialism, and even about the Soviets. Moreover, the editors' distrust of parliamentary gov-

5. Hoffman, *The Twenties*, pp. 6–7.

ernment often expressed itself in attacks upon imperialism and Wilsonian idealism, and these attacks were congenial to many of the intelligentsia. Also congenial, at this point in history, were the journal's pro-German sentiments and the tone of its satire, which exposed the daily practices of statesmen as inane.

In literature and the arts the magazine was even more expressive of the whole liberal social consciousness of the hour. The connection between the political radicalism of the paper and the literary radicalism—of Brooks, for example—with its socialist sympathies, was a loose one and partly contradictory in temper, but both attitudes were motivated by a belief that politics and literature should confirm each other, and both took color and urgency from the revolutionary temper of the times.

Cementing the two points of view and reaffirming the desire of the *Freeman* "to serve disinterestedly its age," was an announced policy of radical criticism of cultural matters in general. This commitment was filled by an unusual richness and variety of writing about institutions and movements. Pervasive in this criticism was the historical and sociological spirit which we associate with such thinkers as Veblen, Dewey, and Oliver Wendell Holmes, Jr., and the faith in "empirical research and accurate description" which characterized their intellectual outlook.[6] And the tone of the writing was marked by that tolerance and humanity we are accustomed to call liberal.

This is not to deny the prejudices and distortions manifested either by the *Freeman* or by the "Enlightenment" of which it was expressive. The paper became known as a "freak magazine"; the period is as famous for its icons as for its iconoclasm. The purpose is rather to suggest how, by its questioning of political and economic issues and its socially oriented literary criti-

6. Hofstadter, *Social Darwinism in American Thought*, p. 145.

cism, this radical magazine brought itself into direct contact with the strong, lively, advanced opinion of 1920.

The first issue of the new magazine came out on March 17, 1920. If it had, as William Dean Howells wrote of *Every Other Week*, "largely put itself together as every number of every magazine does," then the result was most fortunate in its distinctive and unifying effect. Was it by chance, or was it because they relied on the prospectus of the *Freeman*, or was it from a happy journalistic talent for arousing interest that the editors omitted an explanatory editorial on the nature and background of their policy? In any case, laid out on the first page were the staples of their radical theory; the tenor of the whole first number—the substance of the comment on current affairs, the topics of the middle articles, the subject of the leading book review—contributed to an indictment of the state or raised serious questions about the efficacy of political action.

The first *Freeman* dealt with many of the current questions in domestic and foreign politics—the coming national election, widespread unrest in labor, encroachments on civil liberties, the peace treaty, the question of the Soviets, attitudes toward the United States as a world power, the conduct of the Allies. These issues were treated concisely and often sardonically in the paragraphs of "Current Comment" composed by Neilson and Nock, with the assistance of Suzanne La Follette, Louis Levine, and B. W. Huebsch. Nock struck the dominant note, a muckraker's skepticism turned from boards of aldermen to national governments and allied powers. He wrote with scorn of the pretensions of the Republican and Democratic parties, "whose major object" for over forty years had been "to prevent a real issue from being brought before the public," and called upon a coalition of labor, agrarians, and other special disaffected interests "to force upon the country a simple statement of fundamental economic fact—as simple and fundamental, for example, as the tentative program offered them by the Committee of Forty-Eight." [7] (This "fundamental economic fact" was the political economy of Henry George.) Suzanne La Follette carried the charge against governments further, holding them responsible for world-wide labor crises and economic disintegration because they inevitably acted to maintain the rights of monopoly. But "the masses," she continued (with a statement of anarchist doctrine which elicited demands for explanation from several *Freeman* readers),

have never moved toward revolution; they have been pushed. Conditions for which they are not responsible are pushing them rapidly today. A peaceful revolution is still possible and practicable, and such is the eager hope of enlightened minds. The aristocratic state has passed; the middle class state is fast passing, after a much shorter lease of life. The next step, logically, is the proletarian state, whose tenure may be even shorter before the idea of the state is wholly and finally superseded by the idea of Society.[8]

In a consideration of international affairs, Francis Neilson offered, as further examples of dishonesty in politics, the proposals by the Supreme Council for a large international loan to Germany and the documents from the Russian Foreign Office on the secret diplomacy of the Entente, while the "quick and thrifty switch" of Lloyd George to the "daring project of curing bolshevism by trade" was an example of economic realism which put the democracies' moral condemnation of Russia to shame.[9] Nock followed with caustic remarks on the exploitation of Haiti by the United States under the excuse of protection from German influences, and he further developed the theme of political hypocrisy by commenting on the dis-

---

7. "Current Comment," *The Freeman*, I (March 17, 1920), 1. "Current Comment," many of the other editorials, the "Reviewer's Notebook," and a number of the articles in the *Freeman* were unsigned. I have used the publisher's marked copy in attributing authorship. When the name appears in the text, I have not repeated it in the note.

8. *Ibid.*, p. 1.  9. *Ibid.*, p. 2.

tinctions made by the Supreme Court between good and bad trusts, when cheaper goods were the real point. As a final thrust at government, he called the Eighteenth Amendment an evil "foisted on the country" when the "public was ready to acquiesce . . . in a wholesale nullification of personal rights and a long course of nagging, stupid tyranny." [10] The last item in "Current Comment" struck a softer note. B. W. Huebsch observed that "the Ravels, Ropartzes, and Rabauds, and other tenuous musical emblems proffered by our late associates in the war are silently melting out of our concert programs" and that the reappearance of Wagner, Bach, and Beethoven was a sign that sanity was returning, "slowly, perhaps, yet it returns— one hopes with momentum enough to make some discrimination for art when the next war comes." [11]

Grouped in the next section under "Topics of the Day" were four longer editorials. The first, by Nock, used the Esch-Cummings Transportation Act as an example of the folly of Wilson's administration, an administration which had consistently impressed upon the public

the truth that political government, whether autocratic, constitutionalist-monarchial, or republican, is primarily a device for maintaining and as far as possible deepening, the stratification of society into two classes; a monopolist class and a labouring and dependent class.[12]

As is now becoming apparent, it was Nock who struck the most incisive blows against the enemy, the state. The three editorials which followed were all by Neilson and were, characteristically, milder, fuller of specific information, and more discursive. In one, he analyzed Mr. Asquith's victory at Paisley as a sign of the return of liberalism to the principles of Cobden and Campbell-Bannerman; in the second, he condemned the decision of the Allies not to read the Sultan out of Europe; and

10. *Ibid.*, p. 3.     11. *Ibid.*, p. 3.
12. "The Railways," *The Freeman*, I (March 17, 1920), 4.

in the last, he commented with all the asperity of which he was capable on the tendency of governments to find scapegoats for their own dishonesty. His example was Lenin, of whose eligibility as a scapegoat the politicians were so sure "that they promptly placed upon his head all the transgressions they could think of—enough indeed to clear the whole political cosmos of the iniquity of ages past and to come." [13]

In the middle section of longer, signed articles an essay by G. D. H. Cole [14] made the point that the Soviets, as units of economic organization, irrespective of the fate of bolshevism, "have come to stay" because "they arise naturally among men under present conditions and provide a means of popular self-expression far superior to any secured by liberal 'democracy' of the accepted type." [15]

Under "Miscellany" Nock declared that current journals of opinion were atrociously careless in the use of political terminology; the word "liberal," for example,

brings at once before the imaginative mind a picture of the havoc that would be wrought among editors and copy-writers if our journalism rose to such respect for its glossary as always to get "liberalism" and "radicalism" in the right places. Radicals, liberals, anarchists and communists, all find themselves mixed up with very uncongenial company by our undiscriminating newspapers. . . . Why . . . should the *Liberator*, the *Appeal to Reason*, the *New Republic* and the *Nation* be classified as "the radical" press when not one of them is radical or has ever shown even the feeblest tendency towards radicalism? [16]

A fitting conclusion to the political-economic material in this first number of the *Freeman*, with its picture of a society

13. "The Case for Human Nature," *The Freeman*, I (March 17, 1920), 7.

14. Cole was then Secretary to the Advisory Committee of the British Labour Party and had written the Fabian tract on guild socialism.

15. G. D. H. Cole, "Soviets and Social Theory," *The Freeman*, I (March 17, 1920), 13.

16. "Miscellany," *The Freeman*, I (March 17, 1920), 15.

disillusioned by the official activities of nations but buoyed by a belief in the possibilities for freedom in new kinds of economic organization, was a review of Keynes's *The Economic Consequences of the Peace.*[17] Written by William C. Bullitt, this review presented the book as an example of economic realism, the point of departure for an impassioned sermon on the decline of "bourgeois liberalism." Bullitt expressed in vivid language the kind of response to Keynes which disillusioned liberals were making everywhere. The author, wrote his reviewer,

has turned on the gas in the council chamber of Four. . . . He has revealed the exact methods by which the *vieillard prodige* of France, aided by the Artful Dodger of England, seduced the President and took his weapons and his armour from him, piece by piece, and stripped him naked, and sent him home with only the scant covering of an imitation league of nations to hide his shame. . . . No more truthful picture has ever been drawn. No more tragic acts have ever been recorded.[18]

Bullitt's only reservation was that, although Keynes's economic analyses amply supported his picture of the cupidity and folly of this council, the book placed too much faith in the political force called " 'liberalism' . . . that growth of international good will and generosity," which, now gone out of the world, flourished in the final six months of the war and the first months of the armistice. "The hope of Peace," Bullitt declared,

has passed from liberalism to labour. And there is still a chance that the political parties which draw their strength from the labouring class will become strong enough to force a revision of the Treaty before it produces the starvation of millions and the disintegration of European life.[19]

17. This review, like those in the liberal weeklies, accepted John Maynard Keynes's economic analyses without qualification, but the conservative New York *Times* and the scholarly *Yale Review* took him to task for distorting evidence to gain his literary effects.

18. William C. Bullitt, "The Tragedy of Paris," *The Freeman*, I (March 17, 1920), 18.

19. *Ibid.*, p. 20.

Three articles on the arts—"Broadway and the National Life" by Walter Prichard Eaton, "American Literature or Colonial" by Ernest Boyd, a review by Gilbert Cannan of Henry Festing Jones's memoirs of Samuel Butler—and paragraphs by Van Wyck Brooks on several new publications composed the literary part of the magazine. Although they struck a blow for an intransigent criticism of the arts, especially for a fearless evaluation of American literature, these comments were not what the public noticed first about the magazine, nor were they truly indicative of what was to come.[20]

The first number of the *Freeman* was welcomed by the two liberal journals of opinion, the *New Republic* and the *Nation*, and praised by them for its wit, incisiveness, and substance. The *New Republic* found the tone, in spite of the sobering effects of the austere typography, far from quietistic and compared the new magazine to the West Wind of Shelley, "tameless and swift and proud."[21] The *Nation* wrote that the *Freeman* would "apparently sweeten radicalism with wit and irony until the mixture [becomes] irresistible to everybody but 'that camorra of the right-thinking profiteers' (in Mr. Mencken's phrase) who cling to conservative dullness wherever it can find a printer."[22] In another notice the older magazine found "ground for encouragement and satisfaction" in the new publication as a sign of the reawakening of liberalism everywhere.[23]

20. Later, as more talents and more issues came into play, the cultural side of the *Freeman* asserted itself over the political, but for the time being the new magazine stood out as a spirited journal of public opinion whose politics was something of an anomaly among the already established liberal and radical magazines. This reputation was consonant with the original intention of Neilson and Nock, whose primary interests had lain in the world of affairs and whose announced aim was, as we know, to meet the inquiring spirit of the times by probing "all phases of the international life but especially those of economics and politics."
21. "The Week," *The New Republic*, XXII (March 24, 1920), 105.
22. "Notes and News," *The Nation*, CX (March 27, 1920), 402.
23. *The Nation*, CX (March 20, 1920), 353.

These comments represented the approbation of the intelligentsia, who, finding the *Freeman* provocative and impressive, were attracted to its radicalism as a kind of right-thinking without necessarily recognizing or understanding the peculiar nature of its single-tax economics and its bias against the state.[24]

The first questions readers asked about the magazine were political ones. Lewis Mumford, then in England as a visiting editor of the London *Sociological Review*, wrote, for example, a puzzled but pleased inquiry about the first issue:

Sirs: As a voracious reader of six London weeklies I am happy to see in the first number of the *Freeman* a bland mixture of the best elements in each of them. If your critics should urge that the product is not American—as I myself felt at the first perusal—I can fancy your meeting the objection with an urbane "What of it?" . . . Your opinions are plainly more important than your appearance, and it is because they are not yet patent that I seize upon one of them and beg for a more ample exposition. In a happy editorial paragraph on your first past [*sic*] you note that "a peaceful revolution is still possible and practicable, and such is the hope of enlightened minds. . . ." Obviously behind these brief generalizations a whole sociology lies, and I can conceive of your performing no better service during the next few years than by slowly building up, clarifying, limiting, and relating the ideas of social development that are therein implied.[25]

It was to precisely this process that the *Freeman* devoted much of its political editorializing during the first year of its existence, for questions continually arose concerning the basis of its beliefs: What was meant by its often reiterated reference to

24. The reception of the *Freeman* was clearly a case of radicalism misunderstood on all fronts. The conservative papers identified it with socialism, Bolshevism, and the I.W.W. and condemned its indorsement of Keynes's *Economic Consequences of the Peace*. And the simon-pure single taxers, considering the magazine deviationist, ignored it completely at first.

25. Lewis Mumford, "Letters to the Editors," *The Freeman*, I (March 24, 1920), 34.

fundamental economics? Why, as occasion for commitment to political action presented itself, did the paper refuse to take a stand on practical issues? What, indeed, was its view of the duties and responsibilities of a radical?

What gradually emerged, as the *Freeman* worked out its policy (and derived a good deal of editorial vitality from the activity) was the fact that the editors, in presenting their single-tax and antistate views, drew on a body of political ideas ranging from physiocratic and laissez-faire liberalism and Jeffersonian democracy through Henry George to the theories of Franz Oppenheimer and others of his school, who believed that "the real achievement of the state," in contrast to the idealist's rationalization of it, had been "the exploitation of the majority through the possession of political sovereignty by the minority" from primitive times to the present.[26] The result was not so much a system as a set of attitudes which made of the relatively simple single-tax doctrine at the center of the *Freeman* a complex and essentially conservative position—removed from the actualities of an industrial age.

George's conviction that economic freedom is the basis of human liberty and that this liberty can be obtained by giving men free access to natural resources was stated over and over again in any number of contexts by the editors of the *Freeman*, especially by Nock. But, with the exception of the language and ideas of *Progress and Poverty*, those of Franz Oppenheimer's *The State* appear most frequently in the editorial pages of the magazine.[27] Written in Germany in 1908, Oppen-

26. Barnes, "Some Contributions of Sociology to Modern Political Theory," in Barnes and Merriam, eds., *A History of Political Theories*, p. 363.

27. The following summary of Oppenheimer's book suggests the nature of what was important source material for the editorials and serves to illustrate the body of theory to which they frequently refer. Oppenheimer defines the state as "that summation of privileges and dominating positions which are brought into being by extra economic power."

heimer's book belongs to the literature of German socialism, which, although using the class dialectic of Marx, repudiates his industrial emphasis. *The State*, first published in America in an English translation in 1914, was republished in 1922 by B. W. Huebsch. It was an influential contribution to the theories of sovereignty which, with Bernard Bosanquet's *Philosophical Theory of the State* (the third edition came out in 1920) and Harold Laski's *Authority in the Modern State* (1919) as notable examples, engaged the attention of intellectuals in the early twenties. As a writer whose theories were based on the economic structure of an agrarian society, Oppenheimer

---

Society, on the other hand, is "the totality of concepts of all purely natural relations and institutions between man and man, which will not be fully realized until the last remnant of the creations of the barbaric ages of conquest and migration has been eliminated from community life." Man, he says, in order to live, has two means of satisfying his desires: economic and political—work or robbery. Work (economic) is "an equivalent exchange of one's own labor for the labor of others; while robbery (political) is the unrequited appropriation of the labor of others." In the modern capitalist state Oppenheimer attributes the labor surplus and the consequent exploitation of the workingman not to the capitalist process itself (economic means), as Marx did, but to the vast system of territorial estates, which has deprived large numbers of people of their right to the land and thrown them in desperate competition on the labor market. When this system of estates falls apart, as it has already begun to do, there will be no labor surplus and no economic injustice, because "the laborer himself can form capital and himself become an employer. By this time the last remaining vestige of the political means will have been destroyed, and the economic means will exercise sway. The *content* of such a society (in contrast to the class exploitation of a political state) is the 'pure economics' of the equivalent exchange of commodities against commodities, or of labor force against commodities, and the political *form* of this society will be the 'freemen's citizenship.'" By this Oppenheimer means the ideal society in contrast to the primitive state founded on conquest. Oppenheimer acknowledges the force of George's philosophy but places him as a "social liberal" who believed in the "evolution of society without class dominion and class exploitation, which shall guarantee to the individual, besides political, also economic liberty of movement, within, of course, the limitation of the economic means." See Oppenheimer, *The State, passim*.

was congenial to Georgists. The editors of the *Freeman*, in presenting the rationale of their editorial convictions, often used his historical approach to the state and relied on his distinctions between society—"the totality of concepts of all purely natural relations and institutions between man and man" —and the state—"that summation of privileges and dominating positions which are brought into being by extra economic power." [28] One notices also the rather striking similarity between the very name of the magazine and Oppenheimer's vision of a free world where, the exploiting state having withered away, the laborer, economically emancipated, will enjoy the "Freemen's Citizenship." [29]

Socialism represented to the *Freeman* all those tendencies toward collectivism which, by increasing the power of the state, threatened, economically speaking, individual initiative and, politically speaking, the individual's freedom. The quarrel with "latter-day," or progressive, liberalism was a more complex and subtler thing, for the paper, severely critical of the whole range of opinions which belong to the liberal idealism of First World War days, berated strongly the Wilson administration and the activities of the Liberal party in England after the war and made a special point of separating itself from the point of view of the *Nation* and the *New Republic*. Since the new magazine appealed to the same audience of middle-class intellectuals as the *Nation* and the *New Republic*, and since they had welcomed it as one of themselves, it was particularly necessary that the *Freeman* should make sharp distinctions between its radicalism and their liberalism. Nock outlined these distinctions in a long editorial which was published in the third issue of the paper. His piece, called "In the Vein of Intimacy,"

28. *Ibid.*, p. xiv.
29. *Ibid.*, p. 290. Nock, in a letter to Neilson which was written when the name of the projected magazine was in question, preferred "Common Sense," because he considered "The Freeman" a "little special." See Francis J. Nock, ed., *Selected Letters of Albert Jay Nock*, p. 94.

was a typical example of his editorial manner in the *Freeman*.[30] Referring to the cordial but misleading way in which the press and the weekly papers had introduced the new magazine to the world and especially to the *Nation's* welcome of the *Freeman* into "the field of liberal journalism," Nock found it necessary to "deprecate with all possible delicacy this recommendation to the *Nation's* readers":

the *Freeman* is not a liberal paper; it has no lot or part with liberalism; it has no place in the field of liberal journalism and cannot pretend to seek one. That field, indeed, is so competently served by the *Nation* itself, and by the *New Republic* that it would be a superfluity, not to say an impertinence, for the editors of this paper to think of invading it. The *Freeman* is a radical paper; its place is in the virgin field, or better, in the long-neglected and fallow field, of American radicalism; its special consistency, if it ever has any, will be what it can find in that field.[31]

Failing to identify his radical tradition further and skirting a discussion of the philosophical distinctions between liberalism and radicalism ("the dictionary will do that in half the time and save trouble all around"), Nock proceeded to discuss the "practical" attitudes of the liberal and the radical in relation to political action and economic theory. The liberal, he said, whose idea of the state is "pure conjecture" in contrast to the radical's historical approach, believes that the state can be improved by political methods and is, therefore, "politically-minded, with an incurable interest in reform, putting good men in office, independent administrations, and quite frequently

30. All quotations from this editorial are taken from "In the Vein of Intimacy," *The Freeman*, I (March 31, 1920), 52–53.

31. Whether Nock was referring to single-tax radicalism or to Jeffersonian democracy is not made clear in his editorial or elsewhere in the paper. In his autobiography Nock criticizes the Georgists—Baker, Fels, Howe (all except Herbert Quick and Brand Whitlock)—for their uncritical acceptance of the state as a political power. Herbert Quick, on the other hand, "drew the line of distinction sharply between the idea of *government*, as set forth by Mr. Jefferson in the Declaration and

third party movements." The radical, on the other hand, wants to "strengthen economic organization" because he

sees, or thinks he sees, quite clearly that the routine of partisan politics is only a more or less elaborate and expensive by-play indulged in for the purpose of diverting notice from the object of all politics and political governments, namely, the exploitation of one class by another.

In economic, as distinguished from political matters, the liberal, "recognizing only two factors in the production of wealth, namely labour and capital . . . occupies himself with all kinds of devices to adjust relations between them." The radical, in contrast,

recognizes a third factor, namely, natural resources; and is absolutely convinced that as long as monopoly interest in natural resources continues to exist, no adjustments between labour and capital can be made, and that therefore the excellent devotion of the liberal goes for nothing.

As for the current issues which the liberal calls "the democratization of industry," Nock asked:

What good would possibly come to labour or capital or to the public from democratizing the coal-mining business, for example, unless and until monopoly-interest in the coal beds themselves be expropriated? The miners of England have begun to see this and to shape their demands accordingly. What use in democratizing the business of operating railways, as long as the franchise-value of railways remains unconfiscated?

"It has been very distasteful," he concluded, "to make the *Nation's* courtesy a text for the drawing out of these differences between liberal and radical"—differences which he called

---

amplified by Paine and Spencer, and the idea of *the state* as demonstrated in the historical researches of Gumplowicz and Franz Oppenheimer. I owe him [Quick] a great deal, for our conversations helped me vastly to arrange my thought in an orderly way." See *Memoirs of a Superfluous Man*, p. 123.

fundamental—"but the dishonourable acceptance, even for a moment, of an honourable distinction, would be much more distasteful." [32]

Subsequent inquiries and comments, fed by the *Freeman's* stand on current affairs, showed that its readers were still unsatisfied about the philosophical and practical implications of its radicalism. The *Freeman's* sanction of the opposition of British labor to the Allied campaign against Soviet Russia, its sympathy with direct action, and its picture of Lenin as an economic realist whose government, in contrast to the industrial West, promised to marshal the forces of materialism for the good of the human being—all this seemed to place the *Freeman* on the side of the left. Yet the editors' failure to endorse the party platform of the agrarian Committee of Forty-Eight, the persistent suspicion with which they regarded any form of government control, and their assertion that labor and capital had "privilege" as a common enemy—this, on the other hand, seemed incompatible with what was usually considered a radical attitude.

The questioning of most significance came from the left—from liberals, socialists, and other radicals of various types—and concerned such matters as the editors' acceptance of the framework of capitalism, their refusal to make any concessions to political expediency, and what Norman Thomas called the paradox of "blessings for the economic action of class-conscious labour organizations, and cursings for the class struggle theory on which these organizations operate" issuing from the same editorial mouth.[33]

32. Nock, writing to Neilson in the fall of 1919 about a proposal made by Villard that he return to the *Nation*, said the people at the *Nation* were "kind and friendly," but that the paper's liberalism offered nothing that he had "any interest in producing." The *Nation's* advocacy of trade unionism gets nowhere "because economic rent will devour socialized industry, just as it devours capitalist industry." See Nock, *Selected Letters*, p. 95.

33. Norman Thomas, "A Socialist Answers," in "Letters to the Editors," *The Freeman*, I (Sept. 1, 1920), 590–91.

The job of clarification and controversy was shared by Nock and Neilson. It was Nock who, stylizing, as it were, Neilson's political substance, established the *Freeman's* idiosyncratic "master-know-it-all" editorial tone, as it came to be called. Two examples of their editorializing should complete the outline of the paper's radical position.

In answer to a letter [34] entitled "A Challenge to Radicalism," which was printed in the correspondence column of a June, 1920, number of the *Freeman,* Nock dealt with the charge that unfortunately most radical activity was devoted to "the gay business" of destructive criticism.[35] His editorial brought the political tradition of the *Freeman* into the light. The radical, Nock said, is not interested, as his critic had claimed, in destructive criticism or destructive methods but in the promotion of disinterested thought. In support, he quoted Henry George, "the ablest and most distinguished of American radicals," who said:

> Social reform is not to be secured by noise and shouting . . . but by the awakening of thought and the progress of ideas. Until there be correct thought, there can be no right action; and when there is correct thought, right action will follow. Power is in the hands of the masses of men. What oppresses the masses is their ignorance, their short-sighted selfishness.

With this philosophy in mind, continued Nock, the radical will recognize his first duty as that of schooling himself in the literature of the radical tradition that describes the law of the

34. This letter had said that it was the duty of radicals to "accept the obligations of careful, methodical, and constructive thought." They should develop in theory a new economics and a new political economy —"a technique of organization" with which to deal with "a myriad of practical problems involved in a socialist or syndicalist reorganization and operation of society." The letter, claiming to speak for a multitude, was signed "Gallerius," the pen name of Geroid T. Robinson. Intramural warfare was not uncommon in the *Freeman.* See "A Challenge to Radicalism," *The Freeman,* I (June 16, 1920), 328.

35. All quotations from this editorial are taken from "To Whom It May Concern," *The Freeman,* I (June 16, 1920), 319–20.

"economic fundamental"—the writing of Quesnay, Adam Smith, Richard Cobden, Henry George, Ludwig Gumplowicz, Theodor Hertzka, Franz Oppenheimer, and, indeed, Karl Marx, if one reads the last chapter of *Das Kapital*. Having learned from these writers his lesson in fundamental economics and a theory of political economy which envisions "a society entirely free from class domination and class exploitation . . . which assures absolute freedom of production and freedom of exchange," the radical may criticize contemporaneous social problems in that light. A question such as that of union labor and the socialization of industry, which was of deep concern in 1920, would attract Nock's radical only in an educational way:

Trade unionism . . . as an end in itself does not interest the radical; but as a way to the establishment of the co-operative principle he has great interest in it. Nationalization of coal mines, again, is nothing to stir the radical very deeply; as bringing men into a much clearer view of the economic fundamental, however, it has value which he recognizes and fully appreciates.

A more specific attack on the *Freeman's* political negativism was brought about by its extended editorial controversy with Amos Pinchot on the subject of third-party movements and the use of political measures by the Committee of Forty-Eight. The magazine had declined to support the Committee, even though its platform advocated the freeing of natural resources from private control, because a concession to political action was counter to "true radicalism." Norman Thomas jumped into this dispute between the agrarians by writing a long letter attempting to expose the fallacies of the *Freeman's* brand of radicalism, with its refusal to admit that political action and the political state were necessary concomitants of modern society and that "privilege now is part of the warp and woof of the capitalist system," one not to be destroyed without the other.[36] Thomas's communication in the September 1, 1920, number of the *Freeman* showed that the magazine was at that time taken seriously by socialists.

Neilson's reply to the letter has, like most of his contributions to the magazine, the rhetoric of a speech from the hustings. Writing to the editors of the *Freeman* under the pseudonym of Richard Claughton, Neilson used Thomas's socialist strictures as an occasion for a review of the magazine's whole editorial policy.[37] The philosophy Neilson advanced was almost straight Georgism, applied to the uses of capitalism in 1920. His argument turned first on the semantical differences between Thomas's use of the words "capital" and "privilege" and his own (a favorite controversial device with Nock and Neilson). If capital is "that part of wealth which aids in the production of more wealth" (George's definition), and privilege is monopoly of land values, the two are not inextricable, as Thomas maintains, for many capitalists in England and America have recently acquiesced in the taxation of land values as a measure for destroying monopoly. The state, the agent of privilege, is not synonymous with society, and can be "reduced to a mere administrative force by the expropriation of rent, just what it was before rent went into the private pocket of landlords." The *Freeman*'s attitude towards direct action, such as the "international labour boycott against the white terror in Hungary," was not an endorsement of labor's class-conscious struggle with capitalism and therefore contradictory to its policy; rather "these demonstrations were cited merely as a more effective way of bringing the lesson home to labour of its own power as an economic organization than through any course of political action it could take."

36. Norman Thomas, "A Socialist Answers," *The Freeman*, I (Sept. 1, 1920), 590.

37. All quotations are taken from Richard Claughton, "A Lesson in Economics," in "Letters to the Editors," *The Freeman*, II (Sept. 15, 1920), 14–15.

In conclusion, Neilson dismissed Thomas's statement that even if privilege were abolished, "profit-seeking would remain the normal motive in all business transactions," by saying that in a single-tax economy this was nothing to fear:

Let us assume that Richard Cobden was right when he said in the House of Commons that the abolition of privilege, brought about by the confiscation of rent, would mean that there would be always more jobs than men, and that the abolition of privilege would entail a free competitive system from the basis of production, all through the ramifications of industry, urban and rural, above and below ground. . . . Labour with privilege abolished has nothing to fear, and it will be only too glad to pay interest for the use of capital. A natural law under free conditions will maintain that principle, for the motive of mankind is to satisfy its desires and needs with the least possible exertion. And whenever labour can use capital, that part of wealth that aids in the production of more wealth, to lessen exertion and to save time it will do so. . . . What personal gain under a system of equal opportunity can any labourer fear, when he is assured that he will get the full value of his product?

As a coda, Neilson described a millennium in which man, once more restored to his natural economic rights, would bask in an Arcady, where "abundance and leisure" would enable him to reproduce the "cultural and artistic" benefits which (presumably before the Industrial Revolution) he had enjoyed in Europe for a thousand wonderful years of "architecture, literature, painting, sculpture, music, poetry, and drama."

In striking this last nostalgic note, Neilson had, perhaps inadvertently, emphasized a retrospective quality in the *Freeman's* agrarian radicalism. Lacking the warm, direct reformist feeling of the original, the *Freeman's* version of the single tax had converted George's affirmative program into a mode of dissent from the postwar world in general.

From its "radical" position, the paper took, then, a severe view of both the Wilson and Harding administrations, of postwar liberalism in England, of the pretensions of the League of Nations. It condemned United States imperialism in Mexico, in Europe, and in the Near and Far East, ridiculed the futility of the disarmament conferences, used the treatment of Russia by the Allies as a supreme example of dishonesty and cupidity, and published a series of papers by Nock, "The Myth of a Guilty Nation," which attempted to absolve Germany of war guilt. On the positive side the *Freeman* stood for the Irish Free State, for the new Russia, at least provisionally, and for "direct action" by organized labor.

The most affirmative part of the paper, as far as its treatment of current affairs was concerned, was a strong defense of civil liberties: the weekly editorials consistently supported feminists and racial minorities, and constantly scrutinized and exposed attempts to infringe on individual liberties and freedom of speech of all kinds. The tenor and spirit of the editorializing on the rights of individuals may be illustrated by Geroid Robinson's response to an article by Vice-President Coolidge in the *Delineator* (1921). "Are the Reds Stalking Our College Women?" Coolidge had asked. Robinson's reply began:

It appears to us that socialism, syndicalism, bolshevism and general non-conformity in American universities and colleges is a cloud no larger than a man's hand; and on this account we are somewhat surprised to see that a number of people have now fixed their gaze upon this small discoloration of the firmament.[38]

He went on to cite, as examples of Mr. Coolidge's concern, his charge that a member of the faculty at Wellesley had voted for Debs in the last election, and his alarm at a quotation from the Vassar *Miscellany News* which reported that "Miss Smith was quite favorably impressed by the Soviet Ambassador, and struck by his moderation and intelligence compared to the narrowness of some of the [Senate] committee." Mr. Coolidge

38. "Mr. Coolidge on Direct Action," *The Freeman*, III (June 1, 1921), 269–70.

had forgotten that these college people were acting within their constitutional rights, Robinson pointed out; what the Vice-President really wanted was

a kind of extra-legal persecution that will keep college people from doing the things that the Constitution gives them the right to do. What he asks is direct action in limitation of civil liberty—*direct* action against people who have been speculating mildly upon the possibilities of *political* action and have voted occasionally in accordance with their conscience.

To supplement its presentation of political and civil affairs, the *Freeman* made it a policy to re-evaluate established institutions and to deal with social and economic subjects of many kinds. Much of the writing on these subjects came from contributors, the point being to secure as many timely and significant pieces as possible, even if they ran counter to the beliefs of the *Freeman's* editors. "Behind these articles a whole sociology lies," as Lewis Mumford said of the first issue of the *Freeman*. The magazine printed, for example, an appreciation of John Reed by Lincoln Steffens; "The Failure of Liberal Idealism," by Simon Patten; an essay on Daniel De Leon by Sylvia Kopald; an anthropologist's evaluation of theories of the state by R. H. Lowie; "Spencerian Philosophy in 1920," by A. A. Goldenweiser; an essay in praise of the social conscience of Romain Rolland by Gregory Zilboorg; an analysis of the sources of power in modern society by Bertrand Russell; "Why the League Has Failed," by Robert Dell; a series of articles by Sylvia Vana on American education, pointing out its dilution by commercialism; a contribution to an understanding of direct action by Louis F. Post; a description of the psychology of the British working man by Arthur Gleason; an article on the German revolution of 1918 by William Z. Foster; an analysis of Russia's war debt by Michael Farbman; "The Diary of a Casual Laborer," by Powers Hapgood; "Lessons in Revolution," by George W. Russell (A. E.), on the Irish Free State; "The

New Cock-Pit of Europe," by W. N. Ewer, describing the dangers of the partition of the Austro-Hungarian Empire; and five articles by Thorstein Veblen: "Bolshevism and War," "The Captains of Industry," "The Country Town," "The Independent Farmer," and "The Timberlands and the Oil Fields."

Sharing in developing the editorial line, in keeping the paper *au courant* with politics, and in writing more generally on cultural subjects, Suzanne La Follette and Geroid Robinson did extensive and able service, as did Harold Kellock after he joined the editorial staff in 1923. During its four years the *Freeman* maintained a political section which was spirited in style, varied in its coverage, and notable for its inclusion of lively, intransigent material on political, social, and economic subjects. Yet, the course of its prestige as a political organ was downward. Neilson contributed little to the week-by-week running of the magazine after its first year; his withdrawal meant a falling off of interest in English affairs and a loss of concreteness. Nock's stylized reassertions of the fundamentals of Georgism—the thesis that only a sound understanding of man's rights as a land animal could save either American democracy or American literature—took on the quality of a party-line Communist's mechanical reference. People were bored and said so. The theory of the state fared better. The final clarification of the magazine's position against "political government" (carefully defined as not a "mode" but a "genus," having all the properties of conquest and exploitation which Oppenheimer attributed to it) came in a series of articles, "The State," which Nock contributed to the *Freeman* in the summer of 1923.[39] Presented as a clarification of Oppenheimer, these essays were directed toward the postwar world by identifying the French government in the Ruhr with the state and speculating that Russia might possibly develop into a free so-

39. Albert Jay Nock, "The State," *The Freeman*, VII (July 4, 1923), 393–94.

ciety. The essays were regarded by the *New Republic* as a significant contribution to an important and timely subject; they can be taken as an indication of the *Freeman's* debt to a body of sociological theory deemed valuable in the period and of the paper's contribution to the clarification of that theory.

As an editorial policy, the *Freeman's* radicalism held the attention of the intellectual left for a while because Georgism, although it was losing, had not quite lost cogency in the period of industrial expansion and the growth of Marxism following the war and because the political and economic spirit of the paper was in accord with the liberalizing social temper of the hour. The philosophical anarchism of the editors manifested itself, for instance, in many sharply amusing criticisms of domestic and international political chicanery which fitted the mood of postwar disillusionment, and their stressing of economic principles and general championship of civil liberties coincided with the contrasting spirit of hopefulness. Moreover, the fact that the specifically single-tax editorials were set against a rich background of articles on other social subjects added to its power as a significant political magazine.

But, while the editors' program of disinterested criticism appealed in one way to the Encyclopedic temper of the hour, it failed to satisfy it in another, for at the turn of the twenties a quite genuine desire for social action accompanied the thirst for knowledge. In denying politics, as Van Wyck Brooks has said, the magazine ruled out one of the major human interests.[40] Once its radical position was clarified, it could only damn, in different contexts, a whole important world. The result was that the *Freeman* became known, as far as its editorial position was concerned, as a mannered and brilliant freak. One reliable critic of contemporary radicalism, George Soule, observed in

40. This point was made in an interview the author had with Van Wyck Brooks in May, 1950.

1922 that the *Freeman,* viewed in the light of such practical movements as socialism and communism, or labor unions like the Amalgamated Clothing Workers, or the Non-Partisan League, was not a radical magazine at all:

There is . . . a brilliant magazine in New York which takes exquisite pains to inform the reader that it is radical. In precise columns of elegant type, Puritan in its scorn of passion or sensation, it weekly derides the sentimental liberal for ignorance of "fundamental economics." Not long ago it made the startling discovery that Socialists favor taking natural resources out of private ownership. And its "fundamental economics," whenever they appear in language simple enough for the common reader to understand, turn out to be nothing more dangerous than that respectable and ancient heresy, the single tax.[41]

The tartness of this comment, seconded by other sarcastic remarks about "fundamental economics" which turned up after 1921, speaks for the fact that the magazine, once its economic and political policy became clear, could not look for its political constituency among the younger members of the intelligentsia and, indeed, suggests that these readers thought they had somehow been rooked. Placed in an article devoted specifically to radicalism in America, Soule's description of the *Freeman* does not elaborate on those qualities which made it "brilliant" in the eyes of its contemporaries, nor does it discuss the ways in which it did express the spirit of the period. His remark, like the other satiric comments, seems to have been directed specifically to the editorial line established by Nock and Neilson, the original *raison d'être* of the paper, the feature which established it in the period as a "sport."

41. George Soule, "Radicalism," in Stearns, ed., *Civilization in the United States,* p. 273.

# Chapter Three

# Leadership and Letters: Background

In June, 1921, the *Dial* announced an award to be given annually to a young American writer for services already rendered to American letters and as an encouragement to future work. The honor, accompanied by a stipend of $2,000 to provide a year's leisure for writing, was intended, the *Dial* later explained, as a recognition not only of the economic difficulties which beset the writer in America but also of the need to establish "a new relation between the American creative artist and the American people." [1]

During the lifetime of the *Freeman* (1920–24), awards were made by the *Dial* to Sherwood Anderson (1921), to T. S. Eliot (1922), and to Van Wyck Brooks (1923). The writing of these men represented to the *Dial* a contribution to the development of a new, powerful, and disciplined literary consciousness in America. Because this magazine of all the intellectual reviews of the early twenties kept in closest touch with the new literary life and because it succeeded in being experimental without being extravagantly esoteric, its standards of taste come close to forming the literary canon of the period as we know it today. The award itself, therefore, the conviction behind it, the choice of the recipients, and the reasons for that choice may be taken as a key to an understanding of the major tendencies in American criticism and imaginative literature which, having originated in the previous decade, were finding their fulfillment after 1920. Like the other magazines of the intelligentsia, the *Freeman,* in describing and interpreting

1. "Comment," *The Dial,* LXXII (Jan., 1922), 116. The *Dial* stipulated that the recipient must have published in its pages. See "Announcement," *The Dial,* LXX (June, 1921), 730–32.

these tendencies, established its character as a literary journal. And because it had as its chief critic and reviewer Van Wyck Brooks, it made a particular contribution to that strain of criticism which was social, that is, concerned primarily with the status of the writer in America and his relation to American culture.

The question of the status of the artist (most frequently presented as the writer) and the place of the creative arts in American life had been at the center of the avant-garde criticism of the literary generation which, emerging in the early years of the previous decade, had reached maturity at the time of the *Dial* award, and, like the editors of the *Dial*, the critics of this generation had all in one way or another been determined to establish a "new relation between the American creative artist and the American people."

"No one can be more aware than ourselves of the 'untouched reservoirs' of indifference and hostility to any manifestation of the artistic spirit in America," wrote the *Dial*'s editors, as they proceeded to define the cultural situation in the United States. "Centuries of civilization have given other countries a relatively greater number of people who care with more intensity [than do Americans] for art as a portion of civilized existence." The minds of the American people, on the other hand, are diverted from art because they are "cluttered with trivial and ugly things." Since the artist in a civilized country is certain of his place, he is "assured, before he utters his first word, of attention and intelligent criticism," and, unlike the American artist, who must develop "in relation to . . . commerce and publicity," he is spared the "destructive conflict with things which when they are conquered cannot serve him." [2]

The development of any artist's work is determined by his contemporaries, the demands they make upon him no less than

2. "Comment," *The Dial* LXXII (Jan., 1922), 116–17.

the "freedom they allow him in selecting the mode of his response" to the society around him. "America," the *Dial* concluded, "for many generations, has been neither generous in its liberties nor notably severe in its requirements." The award, therefore, is intended as a testimony to the "creation of an attentive and critical environment, receptive and demanding." [3]

The *Dial's* version of the American creative artist "alienated" from the American people was derived from a set of assumptions which had begun to take shape some ten years before, when a new criticism sought to tap economic, psychological, and artistic forces stirring beneath the surface of an established commercial culture. Randolph Bourne, Ezra Pound, H. L. Mencken, and Van Wyck Brooks had all exposed the split between a materially-minded America and its official (genteel) art on the one hand and the "true" artist, the man of spirit, of sensitivity, of intellect (in the Emersonian sense) on the other. "America of today," wrote Ezra Pound in 1912, "is the sort of country that loses Henry James and retains to its appreciative bosom a certain Henry Van Dyck." [4] But Pound also expressed the spirit of the decade when he declared his belief that his country was on the eve of a risorgimento:

This will have its effect not only in the arts, but in life, in politics, and in economics. If I seem to lay undue stress on the status of the arts, it is only because the arts respond to an intellectual movement more swiftly and apparently than do institutions. . . .

A Risorgimento implies a whole volley of liberations; liberations from ideas, from stupidities, from conditions and from tyrannies of wealth or army. [5]

3. *Ibid.*, p. 117.
4. Pound, *Patria Mia*, p. 47. Parts of the book first appeared in London in 1912 in Alfred Orage's *New Age*. The manuscript of *Patria Mia*, submitted to a publisher in the same year, was lost until 1950.
5. *Ibid.*, pp. 41–42.

In describing the nature of this movement, Pound had asserted one of the early and major premises of its criticism, that its basis was humane (in contrast to the sterile separation of genteel criticism from "life") and that it assumed an organic relationship between the arts and the other forces of a culture.

By the time of the *Dial* award two important critical positions had evolved from this premise: the social criticism of Randolph Bourne and Van Wyck Brooks, who thought of the artist in Walt Whitman's sense as the leader and prophet in a democracy and invented for America the idea of an intelligentsia, and the criticism of which Pound was the instigator and T. S. Eliot the coming chief spokesman. This criticism, although it considered new modes of expression as having a dynamic relationship to the modern world, laid primary stress upon the work of art itself rather than the circumstances of its production.

Alfred Kazin has spoken of America's need to rewrite "The American Scholar" every generation. Certainly the avant-garde critics of this twentieth-century renaissance felt such a need. And whatever their diverging points of view, they shared a preoccupation with the question of America's cultural situation in relation to Europe and to her own American past. While their tones varied—Pound writing with more love of country and more sense of the actual texture of American life and language than the rest, Brooks with more pessimism and more flair for the drama of ideas—their tendency was to idealize Europe and to search for a viable native tradition in what they considered a sometimes austere, sometimes raw, sometimes intellectually undeveloped cultural heritage. Thus, in contrast to its more vibrantly nationalistic, more philosophically powerful nineteenth-century counterpart, this later national awakening placed its accent not on youth but on age and maturity.

Europe, in general, represented fulfillment, an old and rich civilization in which an indigenous and highly developed art had evolved as an integral part of the national life—the ideal state which America would achieve when she "came of age." Many shades of feeling in the national consciousness of the decade would account for this. There was the disgust with what Mencken called "the fundamental flabbishness, the intrinsic childishness" of the prevailing moral idealism and with the bloodlessness of the literature which expressed it. Disgust too with the servility to the literary standards of English Victorianism, which Randolph Bourne castigated so vividly. And on the positive side were the romantic appeal made by the art and architecture of Europe to several generations of American travelers and a profound respect for Europe's great nineteenth-century writers. For Mencken America's coming of age meant the cultivation of skepticism; for Bourne, the abandonment of a colonial spirit and the learning of a new internationalism through identification with radical movements abroad. It was Brooks's classic analysis of high-brow and low-brow, his picture of America as an "atrophied personality," divided between the "acquisition of culture and the acquisition of money," which gave the necessity for change its most psychological, most vivid expression.[6] America's cure, he wrote, could come only through the mediation of a great national artist, one who could stir her as Nietzsche and Heine had stirred Germany or Matthew Arnold and Wells, England.[7] Pound envisioned America's cultural unity, her maturity, as a city:

America, my country, is almost a continent and hardly yet a nation, for no nation can be considered historically as such until it has achieved within itself a city to which all roads lead, and from which there goes out an authority.[8]

6. Brooks, *America's Coming-of-Age*, p. 182 (*Three Essays on America*, p. 112).

7. Brooks, *America's Coming-of-Age*, pp. 171–72 (*Three Essays on America*, p. 105).

8. Pound, *Patria Mia*, p. 21.

And, as an observer who understood Whitman's conception of organic art, the word one with the thing, Pound found the first signs of his country's achievement of nationhood in the architecture of New York—expressive of that feeling for property and utility so strong in the American people. "In these new buildings," he said, "the mire of commerce has fostered the beautiful leaf." [9]

When these critics considered their own cultural tradition, they were likely to see it simply, to cast it into the mold of their own generation, to discover in it names and symbols for the qualities they found lacking in themselves. (For example, all the odium heaped on the term "Puritan," which arose from a disgust with the prudery and hypocrisy of the middle-class morality of the day.) In their somewhat lugubrious search for a "usable" past, it was natural that they should turn to Walt Whitman as a sympathetic subject, for he came near to symbolizing the new sense of freedom of their time. Had he not made his own revolt against a genteel tradition, and could he not be the measure of the strength and weakness of America, past and present? Whitman, Pound said, was the prophet of a nation; but "he came before the nation was self-conscious or introspective or subjective; before the nation was interested in being itself." [10] To both Brooks and Pound, who expressed themselves characteristically on this subject, Whitman was like the best in his culture—young, proud, humane, but undisciplined and incomplete. Brooks, looking for a prototype of the artist leader "to articulate the entire living fabric" of America, found Whitman right "on the plane of instinct," but wanting on "the plane of ideas," noncritical and passive as regards the world of established institutions.[11] Pound, his interest ever on the writing itself, heard in Whitman the American

9. *Ibid.*, pp. 27-28.     10. *Ibid.*, p. 64.
11. Brooks, *America's Coming-of-Age*, pp. 121-23 (*Three Essays on America*, pp. 85-86).

keynote but could only consider him an incomplete artist because he lacked "reticence and restraint," the ability to master "the forces that beat upon him." [12]

Pound would surely have seconded Brooks's statement that Whitman failed as a "leader," an artist-critic, because he had not realized that "discipline is, for Americans, the condition of all forward movement." [13] To see any new intellectual movement in terms of liberation and discipline is perhaps necessary to its criticism, although the perspective shifts at different stages within the movement itself. But these twentieth-century critics were restive under a culture which seemed to menace the spirit not only in the larger ways of experience but by a particular looseness and pettiness. So complacent in ideas and so conventional in forms did this culture seem, that to react against it meant coupling discipline with liberty as twin energies in critical leadership from the first. What their own renaissance needed was a criticism which, having exposed the deadness of the genteel tradition, could define and support the genuine artist, direct him to the sources of his strength, and prepare for him a critical and receptive audience. It was in their interpretation of these common aims that the two schools of criticism mentioned above, "the social," and "the aesthetic," began to emerge, as the differences inherent in the imaginative faculties of the critics themselves took on a more definite shape. There was the tendency of Brooks and Bourne to see a culture in relation to a whole intellectual class, and the tendency of Pound to see a culture expressed in the form and texture of its art. In point of time and general public readiness, Brooks and Bourne came first.

In *Letters and Leadership* (1918), Brooks had said that "only where art and thought and science organically share in the

12. Pound, *Patria Mia*, p. 47.
13. Brooks, *America's Coming-of-Age*, p. 126 (*Three Essays on America*, p. 88).

vital essential programme of life can the artist and the thinker and the scientist find the preliminary foothold that enables them properly to undertake their task." [14] This was the principle which he and Bourne had shared in developing a cultural criticism whose focus was literature but whose aim was to force Americans to think newly about all aspects of their culture. Randolph Bourne, whose forte was to identify and then describe, in all their particular deadness, the dead spots in the educational, literary, and political life of his time, had come to believe that the emergence of a whole new intellectual class was a necessary preliminary to the growth of a native art as the highest expression of a "mature" culture. [15] To be formed by an alliance of young students and artists (the "young intellectuals") with "awakened elements in the labor groups," this new, *literary* radical movement would have, as Brooks said, all its predecessors, the muckrakers, had lacked: the "tang and fire of youth," the "fierce glitter of the intellect," a "realistic sense of American life." [16] It would think of culture as a "living effort, a driving attempt both at sincere expression and at the comprehension of sincere expression wherever it was to be found." [17] And the ideal would be a society "democratic in economics, aristocratic in thought." This is Brooks's phrase, which perhaps can be illuminated by Bourne's climactic ending to his intellectual biography of a young literary radical whom he called Miro:

When [he] sees behind the minds of *The Masses* group a desire for form and for expressive beauty, and sees the radicals following

14. Brooks, *Letters and Leadership,* p. 20 (*Three Essays on America,* p. 127).

15. Dupee, "The Americanism of Van Wyck Brooks," *The Partisan Review,* VI (Summer, 1939), p. 75. I am indebted to this excellent essay for its assessment of the idea of an intelligentsia in the criticism of Bourne and Brooks, as well as for its account of the intellectual temper of the period in which they wrote.

16. Bourne, *History of A Literary Radical,* p. xxiii.

17. *Ibid.,* p. 26.

Jacques Copeau and reading Chekhov, he smiles at the thought of the American critics, young and old, who do not yet know that they are dead.[18]

It was for Bourne to write the sociology of this new class, and for Brooks, especially in his later work, to treat one element of this class as "the writer." Sharing his friend's opinion as to the importance of such a class to American society, Brooks, in *Letters and Leadership*, presented to the members and potential members of this new intelligentsia his program of "an organized higher life": "a literature fully aware of the difficulties of the American situation and able, in some sense, to meet them"; a recognition that poets and novelists and critics are the "pathfinders" of society, providing "the vision without which the people perish"; a class (similar to the student class of Europe) "united in a common discipline and forming a sort of natural breeding ground for the leadership that we desire." [19] From this perspective Brooks narrowed the focus to "the writer," exploring the moral, social, and psychological implication of his "vocation"; and, setting against the American situation the ideal of the creative life as exemplified in the European literature of his time, Brooks came more and more to present his subject in terms of failure rather than success. By 1921, the year of the *Dial* award, he had, as creator, synthesizer, and phrasemaker, given powerful expression to all save one of the critical perceptions of his decade. *America's Coming-of-Age* (1915) had defied the present, renounced the past, and described the possibilities of a new culture. *Letters and Leadership*, three years later, had exalted the role of the artist and defined the circumstances conducive to his free and intelligent development. And the *Ordeal of Mark Twain* (1920) had restated, almost obsessively, the themes connected with American materialism and the "alienated" artist.

18. *Ibid.*, p. 30.
19. Brooks, *Letters and Leadership*, pp. 119–24 (*Three Essays on America*, pp. 184–85).

The critical perception lacking was "the aesthetic." Although Brooks had made much of craftsmanship in the context of discipline and dedication, he had used the word morally, not technically; he had done little to distinguish the craftsmanship of the poet from that of other humanists, the philosopher or the historian, for example. As a result, while he had immeasurably furthered the concept of literature as power, so needed in his decade, he had been unresponsive to those tendencies (also needed) in the writing of the period to experiment with language, structure, and subject matter as an expressive whole and as a special kind of truth.

Whitman's remark that he sometimes thought that *Leaves of Grass* was only a language experiment implies a critical principle which required a sensibility different from Brooks's to reformulate for his own generation. Pound, on the other hand, could write of the kind of poetry published in the New York magazines of 1912:

Any pleasant thing in symmetrical trousers will find a purchaser. . . . There is no interest whatever in the art of poetry as a living art, an art changing and developing, always the same at root, never the same in appearance for two decades in succession.[20]

Later in the same essay he expressed a credo that, in the connection it made between honesty and technique, might have steadied American criticism ten years later when "the social criticism" was being decried in favor of the "drenching discipline" of "aesthetic thought" [21]—and when Brooks and the *Freeman* held back from the direction Pound had pointed out:

The force of a work of art is this, namely, that the artist presents his case, as fully or as minutely as he may choose. You may agree or disagree, but you cannot refute him. . . . If his art is bad you can throw him out of court on grounds of his *technique*. Whether he be "idealist" or "realist," whether he sing or paint or carve,

20. Pound, *Patria Mia*, p. 46.
21. Munson, "Van Wyck Brooks: His Sphere and His Encroachments," *The Dial*, LXXVIII (Jan., 1925), 42.

visible actualities as they appear or the invisible dream, *bad tech-nique is "bearing false witness."* [Italics added.] [22]

By 1920 the two "uses" of criticism were, in a manner of speaking, suspended in the intellectual atmosphere of the new decade. Whatever their imaginative or critical inclinations, the critics of the preparatory years had worked assiduously for a new kind of consciousness in the American people and for a literature to give it expression. To think of this conscious-ness as the kind of self-realization which comes from freedom and discipline together, and to think of it as having to be won with extreme difficulty, wrested as it were, from a machine civilization, was almost axiomatic to them. Iconoclasts and en-thusiasts, these critics had also committed themselves to an ex-amination of "the object as in itself it really is." Hence "the fierce glitter of the intellect"; hence the imagist creed. There had been much to accomplish. But the time for propaganda was almost over, and the new intelligentsia were calling for a strengthening of the forces already released. To this the *Dial's* award, symbol of the need of a "receptive and demand-ing" audience, attests. Brooks had often asked for as much, but the concept was coming more and more to mean that the solution to the artist's alienation from the people lay not just in their recognition of him as a moral and creative force; it lay also in understanding his technique, in being initiated into the discipline of his art.

Critical comment and the special citations at the time of the annual *Dial* awards—first to Sherwood Anderson in 1921 and successively to Eliot and Brooks—reflect the changes and counterchanges in attitudes during the years at the turn of the decade, when the *Dial*, the *Nation*, the *New Republic*, and the *Freeman* were leading literary opinion in America. To find Anderson's significance in the fact that he had won "for him-self and for the American people, out of whose life he writes,

22. Pound, *Patria Mia*, p. 77.

a stage of consciousness to which they had not yet arrived";[23] to praise Eliot because he had done much to make clear the relation between the creative artist and the critic, and to put to rout the journalists "who wish critics to be forever concerned with social laws, economic fundamentals, and the science of psychoanalysis";[24] and then to honor Brooks because, "far removed" as he was from "the purely aesthetic attitude," he believed that "the creative life was the only life tolerable to intelligent men and women"[25]—this was, in effect, to convey the tone and texture of the mature years of the criticism that had come into being a decade before.

During these mature years of the awakening the *Freeman* gave the strongest expression among American periodicals to the social criticism formulated by Brooks and Bourne, just as the *Dial*, during these same years, gave the strongest expression to the aesthetic. In their prospectus for the new magazine, the *Freeman's* founding editors had announced a program of "sound criticism, freely expressed, upon literature and the fine arts" as well as offering American and foreign works of the "creative imagination." As the program began to materialize, reinforced as it was by numerous articles on a wide range of cultural subjects, it became apparent that here was a kind of explanatory cultural avant-gardism, designed for the new intelligentsia and dedicated to bringing America to that state of maturity so much discussed the decade before. Here also America was measured by Europe according to the standards then described.

The center of this cultural criticism was literature: the sec-

23. Mary Colum, "Literature and Journalism," *The Freeman*, IV (Nov. 30, 1921), 281. This essay was recommended to readers by the *Dial* in explaining the award. See "Comment," *The Dial*, LXXII (Jan., 1922), 117.

24. "Comment," *The Dial*, LXIII (Dec., 1922), 685–86.

25. "Comment," *The Dial*, LXXVI (Jan., 1924), 96–97.

tion on books (to which the magazine soon allotted as much space as it did to politics), frequent middle articles on matters pertaining to literary criticism, and the essays of Van Wyck Brooks, published under the title "A Reviewer's Notebook"— which gave the literary, indeed the cultural material as a whole, a continuity and a tone unusual in periodical journalism.

Although Brooks played the most important part in formulating the *Freeman's* policy in letters, his was not the only guiding hand. He writes that Albert Jay Nock was responsible along with him, that the other editors were also concerned, and that, in fact, "the whole magazine was in feeling literary." [26] Considering the democratic organization of the staff and the fact that the editors thought of themselves as writers—amateur, not professional, journalists—it is understandable that this should be so and that the conception of literature should have been so broad and so varied.[27] Understandable too that the editors made a virtue of the art of criticism. They all enjoyed doing different things. Albert Jay Nock took on "A Reviewer's Notebook" during a period of six months when Van Wyck Brooks was away on leave of absence. In addition to writing editorials and special articles on political and economic subjects, Geroid Robinson wrote, for example, a series of sketches of "Up State" rural life; and Suzanne La Follette wrote pieces on art. Nock, Neilson, and B. W. Huebsch produced vignettes and comments on music.

Actually two generations of taste were represented on the board: that of Nock and Neilson, which was nineteenth-century and belletristic, and that of Brooks, whose imagination helped to found a new literary sensibility. Both kinds of taste found expression on the magazine, and being closer to

26. From a letter from Van Wyck Brooks to the author, January 18, 1954.

27. Brooks says in *Days of the Phoenix:* "Like Steiglitz, for his gallery, Nock might have said that the *Freeman* was not a magazine, he was not an editor himself, and his writers were not writers." See p. 53.

each other than to what was in the current sense "aesthetic,"
they worked somehow together, to the effect that, while the
*Freeman* assumed a prominent place as an intellectual review,
it never became an outlet for new developments in creative
literature, nor did it often speak the language of criticism which
Pound had used earlier and which became a distinguishing feature of the *Dial*.

The selection of "works of creative imagination" seems to
have been primarily in the hands of Nock, Neilson, and B. W.
Huebsch, with Nock in final authority. In placing emphasis
on this kind of writing, the *Freeman* was unusual among the
American journals of opinion in the decade, but with the exception of some foreign material—Chekhov's diary and notebooks,
Maxim Gorki's reminiscences of Chekhov and of Tolstoy,
Thomas Mann's *Bashan*, Babette Deutsch's translation of Alek-
sandr Blok's *The Twelve*—there was little of either experimental or intrinsic interest. The prose ran to vignettes and
travelogues, of which Gilbert Cannan's *Letters from a Distance*
and *Letters from a Cousin* were a seemingly endless example.
The poetry tended to be Georgian. There were very few
poems printed in the magazine that would neither scan nor
rhyme. Among the American poets who appeared were Elizabeth Coatsworth, Witter Bynner, R. P. Tristram Coffin, and
Leonora Speyer. On the whole, the *Freeman's* tone in "works
of creative imagination" was conservative, and, as an outlet
for their work, the magazine did little to further the cause
of the new writers.

On the other hand, the program of reviewing was alive and
incisive, deriving strength from new writing talents and, within
the range of its social outlook, instrumental in shaping the
careers of young artists, in forming serious literary opinion,
and in providing a rationale for beliefs about the arts in general. Here again, the whole editorial board contributed to the
making of a policy, but Brooks contributed the most. He was

in charge of organizing the staff of reviewers and of designating the books to be reviewed; except for a period of approximately six months (from May 24, 1922 until January 17, 1923), when he was on a leave of absence to write his book on Henry James, his was the controlling spirit of his department. He gave the *Freeman* its literary line as Nock gave it its political, and he undoubtedly exerted an influence greater than that of any other member of the staff upon its literary contributors and readers.[28]

28. See the announcement by the editors of this change of authorship: *The Freeman*, V (May 22, 1922), 262; VI (Jan. 10, 1923), 431 Nock's place as general editor was filled by Suzanne La Follette.

## Chapter Four
# Leadership and Letters: 1920-1924

Because much was expected of Van Wyck Brooks in 1920, his presence on the *Freeman* quite naturally helped to give it a particular interest to the intelligentsia. As Paul Rosenfeld put it, Brooks had already given leadership and corroboration to a whole group of critics (the *Seven Arts* writers) in their recognition of "the new Freudian psychology" as a means of orienting "the social and subconscious background of art" and in their realization that "every original work of art is to a great degree the evolutionary product of social conditions." [1] And he had helped America "to perform with something of ease the act of judgment upon and reconciliation with its past." [2] Now it was expected that he would apply his critical principles to the changing postwar decade in order to find out and guide by specific comment on their work this decade's best writers and train for them an audience. It was expected, in short, that Brooks's criticism would be as significant to the fulfillment of the awakening as it had been to its inception.

One is tempted to speculate what might have been the course of Brooks's career as a critic if he had continued to do the kind of writing which he contributed to the *Freeman* during his first six weeks as its literary editor. The numbers for these weeks testify that he had intended to be a workaday journalist, writing a good proportion of the paper's full-length reviews and keeping its readers *au courant* with a wide variety of publications in "A Reviewer's Notebook." [3] He wrote long articles, for example, on the letters of Chekhov and Henry James, on Isaac Goldberg's *Studies in Recent Spanish-American Litera-*

1. Rosenfeld, *Port of New York*, p. 47.     2. *Ibid.*, p. 45.
3. This was called for the first week "Some New Books."

*ture,* Edwin Muir's *We Moderns,* and Leon Bazalgette's *Walt Whitman.* He made briefer mention of Walter Lippman's *Liberty and the News,* Theodore Dreiser's *Hey! Rub-a-Dub-Dub,* Oliver M. Sayler's *The Russian Theatre under the Revolution,* James Huneker's *Bedouins,* Katherine Fullerton Gerould's *Modes and Morals,* Carleton Parker's *The Casual Laborer and Other Essays,* and Henry Adams's *The Degradation of the Democratic Dogma.*

But to deal with such material quickly and minutely was apparently not congenial to Brooks's creative temperament. He says in his autobiography that he was never at ease in magazine writing:

It sometimes cost me a week of laborious effort to turn out a single book review. The thought of a deadline paralyzed me; I entirely lacked the presence of mind that an article writer must have, like an after-dinner speaker, and my . . . attempts to earn a living on the *Seven Arts* and the *Freeman* were accompanied by a chronic sense of disaster and defeat. What misery to spend five nights a week sitting up until three o'clock to find oneself represented in print by a wretched composition that seemed to be still half-baked and wholly inexpressive.[4]

Given his addiction to meticulous workmanship and his tendency to focus on issues and men rather than on single works of art, it is not surprising, therefore, that after a short time he began to turn the reviewing over to others and that "A Reviewer's Notebook" became the weekly title for a single, highly polished essay in an earlier vein on the creative life in America. (A selection of these essays was published by Brooks, with a few revisions, in 1932, under the title *Sketches in Criticism.* They form, with the addition of his two previous books on America and his biographies of Mark Twain and Henry James, the canon of his influential "early" criticism.) Whatever his feeling of frustration about his work for the

4. Brooks, *Scenes and Portraits,* p. 219.

*Freeman,* these "Notebooks" were regarded with the highest possible respect for the integrity of their composition by the editorial staff of the magazine and by Miss Taussig, who was in charge of composing the dummy for the paper. Because she felt that it was impossible to cut so much as a line, even a word, of the weekly "Notebook," the last item in the magazine, it was her habit to make the paper up backwards.

After his brief period of reviewing Brooks took up his genuine critical métier on the *Freeman* with éclat, writing for the May 5, 1920, issue a stirring and characteristic piece on the hero as artist. It concluded:

> We have had too much talk in this country about the technique of writing. What we need is a tremendous restatement of the responsibility, the opportunity, of the writer. Who but he can project images of a beautiful, desirable and possible social order, focusing the blind and desultory efforts of other men? Who but he can communicate, amid the weariness and the cynicism especially of these coming years, that sense of the miraculous potentialities of life without which the impulse of progress and movement and change perpetually flags and wavers and loses itself in what Theodore Dreiser calls the "mere rocking of forces"? . . .
>
> If literature is capable of these evocations of the dormant possibilities in human nature—and who denies it?—what an immense opportunity the American writer has, confronted as he is with a society in which only two or three notes of the human scale are ever heard! And at this time, especially, when youth in America is so suggestible! Upon the American novelist lies the task of calling to life the innumerable impulses that make a society rich and significant, of opening up new paths and directing floods of energy that refuse to flow in the old channels. Let him create new heroes on the printed page and they will follow in flesh and blood. Let him begin by conceiving and embodying in American terms and under American conditions the convincing image of the hero as artist.[5]

Here, Brooks's followers must have noted, was the major theme which *Letters and Leadership* had announced two years

5. "A Reviewer's Notebook," *The Freeman,* I (May 5, 1920), 191.

before—the responsibility of the writer to "cheer, raise and guide" ordinary men by showing them, amidst the deadening forces of twentieth-century materialism, the social and artistic potentialities of American life. The tone is similar also to the earlier writing in its powerful rhetorical effects and in its note of disillusionment running under the strong note of faith. The whole passage, with its significant opening sentence, "we have heard too much in this country about the technique of writing," together with the idea of the writer's social responsibility and the indictment of American society where "only two or three notes of the human scale are ever heard" makes a statement of a position from which Brooks was not materially to waver during the four years he wrote for the *Freeman*. From this position he sought to touch and mold the intellectual life of these years, which coincided with the fulfillment of the renaissance of the middle decade; but they somehow finally got away from him. "If literature is not to pass into a long sleep, the prey of a sterile aestheticism that substitutes the means for the end," he wrote in his "Notebook" in the last issue of the *Freeman* (March 5, 1924),

it must re-establish its connection with the labouring body of humanity; it must assume that this body has a purpose and a direction. And the great test of writers today is to discover, among the innumerable crosscurrents of the choppy sea of our generation, the cause that contains the most fruitful germ of the future.[6]

What Brooks contributed to the *Freeman* from 1920 to 1924 was first to maintain and then, as he no longer spoke for *all* that was of importance to the world of arts and letters, to diminish his reputation and influence as a critic.

For the first eighteen months the cultural criticism of the *Freeman*, with Brooks at the center and Harold Stearns and

6. "A Reviewer's Notebook," *The Freeman*, VIII (March 5, 1924), 623.

Lewis Mumford as his right-hand men, was virtually the organ of the "young intellectuals." As such this criticism represented a viable extension into 1920 of the critical activities set off by Brooks and Bourne in the decade before. Standing as much for an ethos as for an actual group of people, the phrase itself was at the beginning of the twenties synonymous with the members of America's avant-garde.[7] Harold Stearns gave them both a definition and a name in his *America and the Young Intellectual*, published in 1921 and composed largely of essays (which had originally appeared in the *Freeman*) on the problems of youth in our culture.[8] Describing as a type the young person

7. The core of the group were the men and women of the college generation of 1912 who had found inspiration and outlet in the *Seven Arts* and the fortnightly *Dial*. (It became a literary joke among the *cognoscente* to point out that many of the "young intellectuals" were over thirty.) But their leadership won the loyalties of a younger generation as well. The phrase itself—one can see why "young" and "intellectual" were fighting words in the terrain of the early twenties—seems to have crystallized the prevalent spirit of revolt, perhaps all the more so because it antagonized philistines and genteel high-brows alike. Cf. Burton Rascoe's *A Bookman's Daybook*, pp. 260–67.

8. The title essay of Stearns's book was first printed in the *Bookman* in March, 1921, as an answer to Stuart P. Sherman's "The National Genius" in the January *Atlantic* of that year. Stearns challenged Sherman's attack on the "un-Americanism" and frivolity of the "young writers" and his assumption that there existed in America's "Pollyanna optimism; prohibition; blue laws; exaggerated reverence for women; home and foreign missions; Protestant clericalism . . . anything a civilized man [could] legitimately call moral idealism." See Stearns, "America and the Young Intellectual," *The Bookman*, LIII (March, 1921), 42–48. Two reviews of Stearns's volume of essays indicate the kind of opposition and adulation it aroused. The conservative Brander Matthews called it "a heterogeny of journalistic utterance . . . [a] trick of reckless overstatement and rash generalization . . . . characteristic of the juvenile highbrow." See New York *Times*, Jan. 29, 1922, Sec. 3, p. 8. Newton Arvin in the *Freeman* declared that Stearns, severe on America as he had been, was not severe enough, for Arvin was skeptical about Stearns's belief that a genuine individualism had characterized America in the past. When Stearns thought of his "New England forefathers who kept their blunderbusses well polished and hung in a conspicuous place

whom America in its present state could not satisfy, Stearns presented him as being

not a genius, yet with a certain competence and a real interest in humanistic things . . . perforce . . . a part of the social and economic and educational machinery of the country, albeit a dissident part . . . interested in politics, in contemporary literature, in the type of university life we possess, in science, in art and the American theatre, in the labour movement. . . .[9]

It was for such dissident humanists that Mumford in the *Freeman* wrote his studies of functional architecture and his pleas for a synthesis of science and the arts, that Stearns lamented the alienating factors in postwar culture, and that Brooks expanded his master essay on the hero as artist in a series of "Reviewer's Notebooks" on the circumstances of the literary life in the United States and the role of the writer in the proletarian movement.

As the leader Brooks was the most powerful and insistent of these critics. His "Notebooks" rolled out—the case histories, either psychological or moral, in the inadequacy of American writing talents; the invocations to the writer to follow the high

---

on the wall, ready for highly individualistic use against the reactions of any too tyrannical Government" as forming a tradition of freedom in America, he forgot, Arvin said, how intolerant "these New Englanders were of Thomas Paine, and, later, of Emerson, Thoreau, Garrison, and Whitman." And while Stearns believed also in the "energetic individualism of the frontier," Arvin considered it only a "shallow individualism of adventure and enterprise, not a sound spiritual one of thought and creation." As for Stearns's hope that individualism in America might reassert itself, Arvin asked: "Is it possible even to think of a society more enamoured of conformity, more cruel towards dissent, more anti-individualistic?" See Newton Arvin, "The Foundering Grandsons," *The Freeman*, IV (Jan. 18, 1922), 451. (The title of Arvin's review was the product of Walter G. Fuller, who wrote nearly all of the headings for the *Freeman* during his editorship. They often gave a sardonic flip to things, not inherent in the pieces themselves, and helped to make the magazine's reputation for wit.)

9. Stearns, *America and the Young Intellectual*, pp. 16–17.

priesthood of art; the descriptions of the provincialism of America (in contrast to Europe) which formed a large part of what F. W. Dupee has called "the prodigious anatomy of the creative life . . . in [Brooks's] early writings." [10] Ambrose Bierce was, for example, one of the many gifted Americans whom the country had turned into cynics. Bret Harte and Joaquin Miller were lesser Mark Twains, who had had to show that literature had a pragmatic value in a postwar (Civil War) world. Lanier was starved by the provincialism of the South; Garland by that of the Middle West. Huneker, who loved indiscriminately everything which suggested the sensuous life of Europe, had been chosen as a kind of scapegoat for the repressions of Puritanism. In a lighter tone, Brooks satirized Hamilton Wright Mabie (in his snobbery and piety the typical genteel critic), who was enough to explain why the critics of the new age "so ardently desire a transposition of the forces in our society, why we believe that the devil has a mission on this continent, and why we welcome the exotic influences of the Old World." [11] Running antiphonally to this strain of writers *manqués* were constant references to the great revolutionary individuals, to Emerson, Thoreau, and Whitman, to Arnold, Tolstoy, Dostoyevsky, Nietzsche and Gide (both revolutionary and supremely civilized), who were the creators of new life in their times. And in middle articles and editorials, as well as in other "Notebooks," were Brooks's responses to more immediate topics of importance to literature, such as expatriation, the Puritanism of Stuart P. Sherman, and the writer and the socialist cause.

Just as the *Freeman* was in politics, during the first year or so, more closely allied with what was vital in the American scene than at any other time of its life, so also was it in litera-

10. Dupee, "The Americanism of Van Wyck Brooks," *The Partisan Review*, VI (Summer, 1939), 75.

11. "A Reviewer's Notebook," *The Freeman*, II (Jan. 12, 1921), 431.

ture. The social criticism of Brooks and his followers was still the strongest and most viable element in letters because it reflected, in politics, the revival of middle-class radicalism which followed the war and, in literature, the most powerful strain in American fiction of the time, the Main Street realism. To bring America to national consciousness by analyzing the organic relationships of the artist and society—this aim of the middle decade continued to occupy the avant-garde. Although the "revolutionary" mood of the "young intellectuals" was decidedly tinged with the need to make a personal revolt against commercial, conventional America, their social outlook took strength, for example, from contemplating the possibilities for cultural freedom in the Russian worker's state and for community as well as individual liberty in Freudian psychology. This intellectual temper, which might be called a kind of socialized individualism, is illustrated in Brooks's *Freeman* essays, where the often repeated indictment of American society for failing to "nourish" sustained talents alternates with strong, clear exhortations to the writer to sustain himself and to be the spokesman for the radical forces in his nation. This temper is illustrated also in that critique of society, *Civilization in the United States* (1922), which was edited by Harold Stearns and inspired by the intellectual activity of the *Freeman* and which, with a tone of high despair, attempted to bring an illiberal America to a knowledge of its social institutions.[12]

12. *Civilization in the United States: An Inquiry by Thirty Americans* was edited by Stearns and contained chapters by a number of regular contributors to the *Freeman*: Lewis Mumford ("The City"), John Macy ("Journalism"), Robert H. Lowie ("Science"), Geroid T. Robinson ("Racial Minorities"), Van Wyck Brooks ("The Literary Life"), Harold Stearns ("The Intellectual Life"), Ernest Boyd ("As an Irishman Sees It"). Stearns describes the genesis of the book in his autobiography. "The new *Freeman,* under Mr. Albert Jay Nock's editorship, intrigued me, because of its tone and its superiority in some respects, intellectually and stylistically, to either the *New Republic* or the *Nation.* I knew Brooks and Mumford and many of the others too. . . . I met almost

The tenor of Brooks's writing for the *Freeman* at this time was undoubtedly influenced by his work on *The Ordeal of Mark Twain* (1920). In this, his first full-length study of an American author, certain tendencies in his earlier criticism had crystallized: his ability to make cultural myths, his use of "the Freudian psychology" for images of frustration and fulfillment, and the implied contradiction in his critical philosophy between the overpowering forces of the environment and the inner necessity of the artist.[13] All of this is reflected in "The Wanderers," at once a timely comment on expatriation and a parable of America's fulfillment, which appeared as a middle article in an autumn issue of the magazine's first year.

Using as prototypes the "superfluous men" who "haunt" the pages of the Russian novelists. Brooks describes the twentieth-century American wanderers (the artists and middle-class intellectuals), "Well conditioned, well brought up, well educated," who seek their cultural ideal in Paris, in the South Seas, in Russia, or at home in the I.W.W.[14] "For American society has developed in such a way that it can scarcely command the allegiance of sensitive men." Instead, Brooks wrote, it has turned them into neurotics:

———————

everybody that was interested in intellectual things—that is, outside the strictly academic circles. And gradually, uncertainly at first, but then more and more specifically came the idea of doing 'Civilization in the United States.' " See Stearns, *The Street I Know*, p. 191. Santayana wrote in the *Dial* concerning *Civilization* that he learned more about the despair of its thirty contributors, many of whom had been his pupils, than about American civilization, but that this could not be "entirely at a low ebb if thirty such spirits [could be brought together] by whistling for them." See Santayana, "Marginal Notes on 'Civilization in the United States,' " *The Dial*, LXXII (June, 1922), 553–54.

13. Robert Morss Lovett, reviewing *The Ordeal* for the *Dial*, wrote that Brooks had created "a morality that might be called Every American." See *The Dial*, LXIX (Sept., 1920), 299.

14. All quotations from this editorial are taken from "The Wanderers," *The Freeman*, I (Aug. 4, 1920), 509–10.

These wanderers of ours, who can not find themselves, who can not fit in, these victims of maladjustment, of every known Freudian complex, are they not visibly manufactured by conditions of our life, economic, religious, educational, domestic, upon which the most casual diagnostician can lay a confident finger?

But, he continued, these victims of America, who have suffered the ordeal of being alienated, are going to redeem their country; by being separated from her, they will have gained knowledge of her, will have learned to know the American people "from within outward, from the bottom up" and to recognize the "unreality of what at present passes for literature, art, and religion." Their "desocialization" will be the first step in the evolution of the true "illuminati." But their knowledge, their light, must be complemented by a realization that they are free to transcend the conditions of commercialism. (Here Brooks has shifted the responsibility from society to the artist and the method from the analytical to the hortatory.) "The road will be a long one," he warns, and the wanderers must understand "that truth is to be found only within themselves."

If they despise America, they will deserve the fate that prevents them from realizing their luminous aims. . . . They are not entitled to bitterness. Having access to the whole world of psychology, philosophy, and history, they are under the free man's obligation to see themselves in the common sunlight. That is what makes the difference between the Maxim Gorky's and "the creatures that once were men."

And, Brooks concluded in the revolutionary vein of Randolph Bourne, the triumph of the wanderers, as well as America's salvation, must come in their social leadership. "It is when the intellectual wing of the I.W.W. begins to produce its Maxim Gorky's that we shall know that the dawn has come."

"The Wanderers" was printed during a lively exchange of views in the *Freeman* on the exodus to Europe, expatriation having already become a moral problem for writers in 1920.

Harold Stearns began the controversy in the August 4th issue. After vilifying America as "late eighteenth-century in government . . . early nineteenth-century in culture and morals [and] of the stone-age in business," he asked, "What can a young man do?" and then gave the inevitable answer—"Get out!" [15] Indignant replies in the "Letters to the Editors" made the points that the young, either out of a sense of duty to their country or in a spirit of combat, should stay at home to make their ideas prevail. Mr. Nock closed the argument in an editorial on September 8 by asking, with his usual scorn of America's mass culture, why, if the majority preferred America the way it was, it should not be allowed to remain unchanged, and why those who did not like it should not do American culture a service by "throwing their powers to strengthen the centers of culture which at present lie elsewhere." [16] But it was Brooks who wrote, in addition to "The Wanderers," an editorial which was the official reply to Stearns. "Go abroad, Carissimo," he said, and as usual he gave his subject a tradition and an inspirational voice:

America, like every newly settled country, has been jealous of its own; its material development required for many years the solicitude of every citizen. That is why, in America, expatriation has become a breach of the tribal law. And that is why all but the strongest Americans who leave their country are constrained to feel themselves deserters. Let them set their minds at rest. We live in a new epoch; the time has come to perceive that through the self-fulfillment of its constituent individuals alone a nation can become great.[17]

Reservations, either direct or implied, about the activity under Brooks's leadership at the *Freeman* in 1920–21 came from several respectable quarters. As a dissenter from within, Albert

15. Harold Stearns, "What Can a Young Man Do?" *The Freeman,* I (Aug. 4, 1920), 490–91.
16. "Culture and Freedom," *The Freeman,* I (Sept. 8, 1920), 581.
17. "Go Abroad, Carissimo," *The Freeman,* I (Sept. 1, 1920), 606.

Jay Nock often objected to the emphasis placed by the "young intellectuals" on "the plight" of the American artist and to the exuberant generalizations of their cultural analyses.[18] The *Dial*, which often spoke jokingly of the stresses and strains of ordealism, was also gathering forces for its strongest condemnation of the failure of the social critics to concentrate on art instead of on the situation of the artist—exemplified by the award to Eliot in December, 1922.[19] The *Nation* had, in Carl Van Doren, a writer who respected Brooks's iconoclasm but entertained some doubts about the fullness of his knowledge of American life and questioned his assumption that "it is after all the prime business of a nation or a period to beget men of letters." [20] Burton Rascoe, from the essentially friendly Mencken camp, pointed out gleefully the difficulty of grasping the meaning of Brooks's nice distinctions about the fate of the writer in America; for example, the statement that "while America fails to nourish the writer, it appreciates the writer, on the whole, if he has been able, in spite of all, to make something of himself, almost, if not quite, in the measure of his deserts." [21]

The two strongest criticisms of Brooks's position came, how-

18. In one essay Nock said that these critics should leave off the victimization of the artist by American society ("a wholly imaginary predicament conjured up by Mr. Mumford") and turn their attention to the problems of a work of art. See Albert Jay Nock, "A Study in Criticism," *The Freeman*, III (March 16, 1921), 406. Nock expressed his views in a series of essays on criticism and incidentally throughout his editorials. His sentiments were those of the "aesthetic" group, but his classical and, as it came to be felt, essentially nonartistic temperament was too far removed from the social and creative sensibilities of the younger writers to appeal to them. Cf. Chapter VI, p. 137. Nock's essays enhanced the liveliness of the *Freeman* by stirring up controversy, and they enhanced its reputation for variety in opinions, but they did not greatly modify the strongly Brooksian tone.

19. See Blum, "American Letter," *The Dial*, LXX (May, 1921), 562–68.

20. Van Doren, "The Fruits of the Frontier," *The Nation*, CXI (Aug. 14, 1920), 189.

21. Burton Rascoe, "Reviewing the Reviewer," in "Letters to the Editors," *The Freeman*, II (Jan. 26, 1921), 473.

ever, from the literary right and the political left—from Stuart P. Sherman, who in 1920–21 was the arch professorial and "Puritan" enemy in the eyes of the social critics, and from Max Eastman, who spoke in the *Liberator* for the Marxists against the liberal ideology of the literary radicals. In both cases Brooks defended to the satisfaction of his followers the literary and political individualism which was the core of his critical philosophy. In taking his stand on issues which were of importance to letters at this time, he succeeded in clarifying his conception of traditionalism and of leadership in the light of the challenges of the postwar world.

Sherman had attacked in the October, 1920, *Bookman* the "young" critics, Huneker, Spingarn, Mencken, Lewisohn, Hackett, Bourne, and Brooks, who were represented in Lewisohn's newly published anthology, *A Modern Book of Criticism*. In his article entitled "Is There Anything to Be Said for Literary Tradition?" he called them "restless impressionists . . . destitute of doctrine," who, having found the English tradition unserviceable and the American "effeminate and over-intellectualized," had turned to the Continent. Could their seeking of "foreign allies," Sherman wondered, come from the leadership of "writers whose blood and breeding are as hostile to the English strain as a cat is to water?" [22] The young modernists, he wrote chastisingly, would be unlikely to "hear any profound murmurings of ancestral voices" in the writings of Mark Twain, Whitman, Thoreau, Lincoln, Emerson, Franklin, and William Bradford, in whom our native tradition, "a vision pressing for fulfillment," is expressed, for the modernists have "a sentimental fondness for representing life as a meaningless surge of base and beautiful forces."

The tone of Sherman's piece seems, even today, condescend-

22. For quotations from this essay see Sherman, "Is There Anything to Be Said for Literary Tradition?" *The Bookman*, LII (Oct., 1920), 108–12.

ing and stuffy, perhaps faintly nasty, in its ridicule of *les jeunes;* it was the sort of writing that infuriated the "young intellectuals," and one can imagine the effectiveness of Brooks's reply, which was couched in his best Arnoldian manner, dignified, reasonable, cogent. Faced with the repudiation of native writers which he had made in *America's Coming-of-Age*, he reaffirmed his belief that America had had no *literary* tradition, but he made a step toward a sounder evaluation of the spirit of the older writers, finding in them the honesty which he needed to counteract the religiosity of his opponent.[23] Young American critics have not, Brooks wrote in an October editorial in the *Freeman*, "wilfully" turned their backs on the American tradition.[24] In seeking literary inspiration in Europe they have simply done what the great American writers have done before them and what the conditions of American literature, past and present, have made necessary. The "modernism" of the newer critics is a necessary revolt not so much against what actually is in the American past as against what the philistines and the genteel critics have found there—moralism, Puritanism, a cutting off of universality which Matthew Arnold had condemned as an enemy to light. "If they [the young critics who turn to European literature] prefer Ibsen and Nietzsche to Messers. Tarkington and Churchill, they may rest assured that Whitman and Thoreau and even Emerson would have approved of them." Emerson indeed had said: "Accept . . . the society of your contemporaries, the connection of events"; he [Emerson] is a "dangerous ally for Professor Sherman," Brooks concluded, "if he wishes to make war on the young."

23. Brooks confesses in his autobiography that when he wrote "so cavalierly" of "Our Poets" in *America's Coming-of-Age*, he had "scarcely read" them, had simply reflected what he had learned at Harvard, where "English authors were always cited in preference to Americans, even when these could also be called classics." See *Scenes and Portraits*, p. 111.

24. For all quotations from this essay see "Professor Sherman's Tradition," *The Freeman*, II (Oct. 25, 1920), 151–54.

"The connection of events," in the shape of the Russian Revolution and the postwar re-examination of middle-class radicalism, had brought into question Brooks's conception of intellectual leadership in the socialist cause. For him socialism had always been less a body of doctrine than a state of mind, an ideal of liberty toward which the artist-critic must lead a people along a journey through knowledge, light, and responsibility. Of this "The Wanderers" was an allegory, and the concept was implicit in all the *Freeman* essays touching on politics. It was brought into action when the formation of a Communist organization of French intellectuals and proletarian revolutionaries (Clarté) under Henri Barbusse, making a bid for international support, aroused comment in American liberal and leftist periodicals. Max Eastman, declaring Barbusse unrealistic because he believed that intelligence could resolve the class struggle, had declined to sponsor Clarté in the *Liberator* and had thereby drawn the line between middle-class and Marxist radicals in America.[25]

In various exchanges between Brooks and Eastman the matter narrowed down to the function of the writer in revolutionary times.[26] Eastman, although he was unwilling to grind the writer in the party mill, banished him from revolutionary activity because he was likely to be either dangerous or frivolous. Brooks defended the writer's power and usefulness as an individual who, in presenting life honestly as he saw it, could bring the American proletariat to intellectual and social maturity. The great socio-democratic tradition in nineteenth-century English

25. For a full account of the position taken by Eastman and the *Liberator* on Clarté, see Aaron, *Writers on the Left*, pp. 52–55.

26. For the *Freeman–Liberator* controversy see the following: "A Reviewer's Notebook," *The Freeman*, I (May 12, 1920), 214–15; Max Eastman, "Clarifying the Light," *The Liberator*, IV (June, 1921), 5–7; "A Reviewer's Notebook," *The Freeman*, III (June 20, 1921), 382–83; Max Eastman, "Inspiration or Leadership," *The Liberator*, IV (Aug., 1921), 7–9; "A Reviewer's Notebook," *The Freeman*, III (Aug. 31, 1921), 598–99.

and European writing was Brooks's warrant for this staunchly liberal position.

When Brooks wrote in an early "Notebook" (May, 1920) that what America lacked was "both a grasp of the psychology of the artist and a sense of the artistic vocation," he was speaking to an understanding, not yet sated, audience; these lacunae his *Freeman* essays had attempted to supply.[27] He had in many of his studies suggested how Freud might be used to orient "the social and sub-conscious background of art," or at least of the artist; he had spoken often, in terms characteristic of his earlier writing, of the disciplines of criticism. If, on the whole, the strain of "ordealism" was stronger than the strain of social responsibility, the tone had not yet turned to gloom. All in all, he had succeeded in "getting under the skins" of many Americans (as Edmund Wilson put it), because his many-faceted analysis of the artist's situation corresponded to the mental pattern of the intellectual in the very early twenties— frustrated by commercialism, torn between America and Europe, intent on asserting his personal liberty, but at the same time drawn toward radical groups, traditionless but wanting a tradition, disturbed by encroachments of science on the arts but fascinated by psychology and the new social sciences, only casually interested in the formal properties of art.

Brooks was still the leader of American criticism when he wrote the *Freeman's* editorial which acclaimed the first *Dial* award; Sherwood Anderson, he said, had begun to fulfill the prophecy of Whitman that " 'the infant genius' of the American literature of the future . . . sleeping far away, unrecking itself in some western idiom . . . would sprout, in time, flowers of genuine aroma." [28] The award sprang from "such a generous understanding of the nature and the conditions of

27. "A Reviewer's Notebook," *The Freeman,* I (May 5, 1920), 190.
28. For all quotations from this editorial see "Current Comment," *The Freeman,* IV (Dec. 14, 1921), 315.

the creative life that it seems destined to have . . . a direct beneficial influence on American letters." The money, in releasing the recipients from the pressures of commercial competition, "virtually . . . amounts to a cordial invitation to the American writer to become, not what other writers are but more and more his unique self."

In 1922 Brooks's rapport with avant-garde opinion and activity began to break, and the change became evident in the tone and tenor of the *Freeman* essays as well as in his critical reputation. To those of his own, the *Seven Arts*, generation, like Rosenfeld and Stearns, and to the younger writers and reviewers also, his failure to deal directly and affirmatively with the literature of the present seemed an increasingly serious default.[29] Even in the period of his greatest prestige on the *Freeman*, he had made little mention, either incidental or otherwise, of contemporary writing, but this lack became more noticeable as the movement in criticism to relate the artist to the structure of postwar society gave way to political apathy and to a concern with the structure and language of literature itself.[30] Brooks's subsequent contributions to the magazine (interrupted by a leave of absence from May, 1922, to January, 1923, to

29. Rosenfeld, *Port of New York*, pp. 57–58.

30. Brooks's most trenchant remark on the subject was a rebuke to Mencken for his uncritical acceptance of the "new," in this case his indiscriminate promotion of Dreiser and Cabell. Describing the ideal of the writer as one who in his "fullblooded and at the same time intelligent individualism . . . never relinquishes the solitary search after his own perfection," he asked: "Does Mr. Dreiser answer to that ideal? In its name one can say that no writer, in the modern world, is entitled, for all Mr. Dreiser's admirable incorruptibility, for all his admirable talent, to go through life as benighted as he. Does Mr. Cabell answer to that ideal? The stagnant gentility of the typical Southerner is written all over his work: one can see with half an eye that his Rabelaisianism is only skin deep." See "A Reviewer's Notebook," *The Freeman*, II (Nov. 24, 1920), 263. Such judgments are tantalizing examples of Brooks's social imagination put to excellent artistic use.

write *The Pilgrimage of Henry James*) were devoted either to an examination of nineteenth-century writers or to a quarrel with the aesthetic avant-garde. These contributions mark what was essentially a period of stasis and review, a kind of stand-pat-ism which suggests that the limits of his imaginative sympathy with his time had been reached.

In writing of Poe, Melville, Whitman, Henry James, and Stephen Crane, Brooks was furthering the movement to establish a new, nongenteel canon of American literature, inaugurated by his own criticism in 1915. The familiar themes of Brooks's earlier studies of American figures occur in these later "Notebooks." Whitman, as was usual with Brooks, is the measure of America, past and present. The several essays on Henry James reflect the question of the émigré artist, which Brooks was to bring to a full development in *The Pilgrimage*. Poe and Crane are presented as types of dedicated artists; Melville's career illustrates "the suffocation of a mighty genius in a social vacuum." [31] But, although the biographical method and the ordealist cast appear in these later essays, one notes that a consideration of technique is introduced, especially in five "Notebooks" on Melville, which review his works in detail and "explore the deliberate art" of a "mighty genius." [32] Why Father Mapple's sermon seems to "build itself into the tissues of our imagination . . . what keeps the fabulous element entirely consonant with reality . . . how the pitch of the book is maintained"—these are the critical inquiries about *Moby Dick*, for example. And the essay sums up the great organic power of the whole, which makes us feel "beneath the book the very pulse of the ocean itself." [33]

Perhaps Brooks's treatment of these American figures was

31. "A Reviewer's Notebook," *The Freeman*, VII (May 23, 1923), 263.
32. "A Reviewer's Notebook," *The Freeman*, VII (May 16, 1923), 238.
33. For all quotations from this essay see "A Reviewer's Notebook," *The Freeman*, VII (May 16, 1923), pp. 238–39.

an answer to the disappointment of his followers that he had not written more specifically about individual writers and their craft.. But the essays, nonetheless, kept their writer on the periphery of developing interests in criticism. To write of figures of the past was modern, for traditionalism was being conceived of in a new way; to write extensively of the art of a single book was also modern. But the degree of modernity turned on what past and what books—and on the excitement and assurance with which the critic met what seemed to be a triumphant burst in literature of unfamiliar and challenging modes of expression.

Because Brooks's critical imagination had shown itself from the beginning of his career as essentially social and ethical rather than artistic, it is not surprising, then, that he should have neglected even the contemporary realists and that he should now quarrel strongly with experimentalism in fiction and poetry.

His comments upon Ezra Pound and his group in early issues of the *Freeman* had been ambivalent but, nonetheless, made perfectly clear the basis of his temperamental disagreement: their writing (the "literature of self-expression . . . the strange experiments of the *Dial* and the *Little Review*") seemed "dangerously private and personal." [34] Pound, Brooks wrote in a review of *Instigations* (1920), "has very much at heart the civilization of these United States." [35] He has the literary vocation: "a fresh wind of the spirit blows from cover to cover." But he has not allied himself "with the most creative forces of our day, the intellectual proletariat." Instead, he "has inhabited for a long time a universe that consists mainly of Wyndham Lewis, Chinese characters, Provençal prosody, Remy de Gourment, Blast, and the Vortex."

34. "A Reviewer's Notebook," *The Freeman*, II (Sept. 15, 1920), 23.
35. For all quotations from this review see "A Review's Notebook," *The Freeman*, I (June 1, 1920), 334–35.

Now, in 1922, an upsurge of experimentalism, indicated by the *Dial's* award to Eliot and its publication of *The Waste Land* and by the activities of younger writers, who were forming literary coteries, founding little magazines, and publishing aesthetic manifestoes, provoked from Brooks and the *Freeman* an unequivocal restatement of his old critical position. The immediate stimulus was, it seems, an editorial in the little magazine *Secession,* calling for "an unemotional sloughing off of irrelevant drains on one's energies and a prompt deviation into purely aesthetic concerns." [36] The writer of the editorial, Gorham B. Munson, recognized the "valuable work of Brooks and Mencken;" but asserted the need of a small group of writers, "able by reason of the different direction of their work," to secede from a literary milieu "which believed that literature was social dynamics and that its social significance was paramount." To this Brooks replied that "it still remains for the critical faculty to make intellectual situations of which Arnold has said the creative faculty may properly avail itself." [37] Admitting that there had been "of late too much flogging" of dead horses, Brooks demurred strongly at the conception of "purely aesthetic concerns":

The formal qualities alone, and especially the "abstract form" of our contemporary cerebralists, will never constitute a literature; and little is to be expected of a criticism that regards them as the weightier matters of literary law.

Unless American criticism can do again for the twenties what it did for the "sociological" literature of the preceding decade,

36. "Quoted in "Secession," *The Freeman,* VI (Jan. 10, 1923), 414. The editorial, which appeared in *Secession,* No. IV (Nov., 1923), was a summary and slight rewording of an article by Munson, "The Mechanics for a Literary Secession," published in the little magazine *S4N,* Third Anniversary Ed. (Nov., 1922). The editor, Norman Fitts, pointed out in a letter to the *Freeman* that Brooks had actually quoted from the original article, not the editorial.

37. For all quotations from the editorial see "Secession," *The Freeman,* VI (Jan. 10, 1923), 414.

Brooks warned, "our secessionists will simply be leaving one wilderness for another."

In a series of "Reviewer's Notebooks," which followed the editorial on *Secession*, Brooks returned again and again to the question of aestheticism in contemporary letters. A concern with the principle of form ("However it may be in the plastic arts, in literature the subject *dictates* the form" [38]) and a concern with the principle of reality in relation to the writer in the postwar world ("An art that is to regenerate reality can only be repelled by reality up to a certain point" [39]) give these essays a certain richness. And warnings in this new context against divorcing art from society reaffirm with renewed vitality the humane aims of the social criticism. Yet, one looks for and does not find an act of the critical imagination which would sort out the genuinely imaginative and "serious" from what was false and trivial in contemporary literature. Instead, the activity of "countless writers" of the day is lumped into a "game," a "sort of learned spoofing." All these writers indulge in spilling out "all sorts of ingenious patterns . . . fetch up tags and tatters of a badly assimilated erudition . . . match unfamiliar quotations. . . ." [40]

Further comments in the *Freeman* followed this same pattern, presenting the contemporaneous literary situation as a place of sterile aestheticism and obscurantism, a Brooksian wasteland where,

especially since the war, there has been a strange growth of cliques and coteries, mutual benefit and protection societies and magazines devoted to the propagation of secret writings. These curious efforts to communicate and at the same time obstruct communication, to court a public that it generally despises, to express and yet refrain from expressing, to substitute a cipher for a language, are perhaps what they profess to be—the most characteristic and the most symptomatic literary facts of the moment; but like the phenome-

38. "A Reviewer's Notebook," *The Freeman*, VII (Aug. 8, 1923), 527.
39. "A Reviewer's Notebook," *The Freeman*, VII (July 25, 1923), 479.
40. "A Reviewer's Notebook," *The Freeman*, VII (Aug. 8, 1923), 527.

non of spiritualism they lend themselves to a very unflattering psychological interpretation. The elements of gregariousness, evasiveness, contradictoriness . . . of which they largely consist, reveal them as very notable signs of . . . insecurity.[41]

In contrast to this phase of a "ravaged, hostile" world since the war, a world that "has ceased to believe in itself," and that offers to contemporary writers no "postulates, moral or social" that they can "uphold" or "react against," Brooks evokes the "organic" literature of the nineteenth century: Melville, Whitman, Ibsen, Tolstoy are "immense windows that open upon vast spaces—continents, oceans, or long visions of history." The twentieth century has vision, but it belongs to the scientists. Writers and workers have fallen apart. To save himself, as did Yeats through Irish nationalism, as did Anatole France through socialism, the contemporary writer *must* "find the cause which will contain the most fruitful germ of the future."

Here, as in "The Wanderers," Brooks had written a prose poem of the twenties. Although directed against "the lost generation," this later piece shows striking affinities with their themes of a fragmented modern world. Brooks could still make myths of contemporary situations, it seems, but he failed to respond to the wastelands of others. And because he did not grasp the form and substance of what was creatively alive in his decade—it was, after all, a vital period—he ceased to be an affirmative critic in the way that affirmation was then understood—as an intuitive response to the integrity of a work of art. Brooks's limitations as his contemporaries came to see them may be illustrated by a comment from Edmund Wilson's review of *The Pilgrimage* in 1925:

Mr. Brooks is a romantic and a preacher and has little real sympathy or comprehension of the impersonal and equanimous writer like James. . . . In the case of James the artistic accomplishment

41. For all quotations from this essay see "A Reviewer's Notebook," *The Freeman*, VII (March 5, 1924), 623–24.

is far more interesting than the man. Henry James was not an in-
timidated and sidetracked artist but a writer who understood both
himself and his society and was signally successful in expressing his
views about them. It is difficult for Mr. Brooks to write anything
about James which James has not written about himself.[42]

But, whatever Brooks's attitude toward contemporary writers
and critics in 1922–24 and their attitude toward him, he was
still regarded as a critic of stature. The *Dial* award to Eliot in
December, 1922, was so phrased as to be a rebuke to Brooks
and the *Freeman*—Eliot should "put to rout those journalists
who wish critics to be forever concerned with social laws,
economic fundamentals, and the science of psychoanalysis."
But the *Dial's* recognition of Brooks himself the following year,
half-nostalgic as it probably was, may be taken as a gesture of
deference to a man of vision, to a valiant pioneer into the commercial wilderness where trees remained to be felled, even
though it seemed likely that these latter-day tasks would be
performed by others. "Far removed" as he is from "the purely
aesthetic attitude," said the *Dial*, "he has believed that the creative life is the only life tolerable for intelligent American men
and women, that the life which is not creative is spoiled and
stunted and unworthy." [43]

Brooks had, indeed, in the *Freeman* and earlier, given to the
artists the image of America's maturity and of themselves.

42. Edmund Wilson, "The Pilgrimage of Van Wyck Brooks," *The New Republic*, XLII (May 6, 1925), 286.
43. "Comment," *The Dial*, LXXIII (Dec., 1922), 686.

# Chapter Five

# A Corps of Reviewers

Brooks believed in 1920 that one of the chief functions of critical leadership in the United States was to rescue American taste from the "limbo" of the conventional magazines which for so many years had kept literature an "adjunct" to business.[1] Developing this theme in one of his "Notebooks," he declared that taste in this country might be transformed "in ten years" if we had a journal of literary criticism "as good as any one of half a dozen European journals [he] might name." [2] Such a paper, the rallying point for the new intellectuals, would "represent a multitude of positive traits of intellect and character . . . not in a single person only but in a group," whose sole aim would be "the sincere and truthful expression of the reality within the American people." He believed that to find a "corps of reviewers" for this purpose, "willing to co-operate in such an enterprise and able to command, comprehensively, adequately, for America, the whole field of human expression" would not be impossible, for new knowledge and insight were abroad in the land. However, there was lacking "the form that makes them tell," American reviewing being torn between "the hideous and detestable neologisms of the newspaper world," and "the gray Johnsonian starch of the tongue of the universities."

These statements, so characteristic of Brooks, bear witness to the spirit in which he undertook his job as literary editor of the *Freeman*, and they testify to that of his colleagues as well.

1. "The Limbo of the Magazines," *The Freeman*, I (July 28, 1920), 461–63.
2. For all quotations from this essay see "A Reviewer's Notebook," *The Freeman*, I (July 28, 1920), 478–79.

Indeed, the sense of new kinds of knowledge mushrooming everywhere was shared by the editors of all the good magazines, who experienced also the difficulties of training eager but raw young critics to express what confronted them. In reacting to these live currents in American culture after the war, in the whole subtle process of attracting writers to its staff, choosing and weighing subjects for presentation, and legislating on the question of form, each magazine evolved a characteristic tone.

Other editors, like Brooks, regarded the question of form as a sizable problem. Among them there was general agreement both that America lacked a well-trained class of professional journalists on the intellectual level of Europeans and that the illiteracy of young neophytes in criticism was appalling. Oswald Garrison Villard, for example, had noted the poverty of his own resources, when he took over the *Nation* in 1918, in contrast to those of the editor of the London *Nation*, H. W. Massingham, who was

in a position no American editor could hope to approach. He was surrounded by gifted and highly trained writers, all of them experts in certain fields, whom he had only to call on the telephone in order to obtain a first class article, admirably written and rarely requiring the slightest editing. . . . It is rare, indeed, that a manuscript reaches the editor of any American journal which has pretensions to style that does not call for much revision, even to spelling and punctuation, unless it comes from England.[3]

Harold Stearns, writing of his editorial work on the fortnightly *Dial* in 1919, says that he was impressed by the paradox of "the incredibly low standard [among young aspirants to a critical career] of literary appreciation and of critical ability prevalent in a country that had so long had the blessing of general education." [4] Touching on the fact that the established

3. Villard, *Fighting Years*, pp. 375–76.
4. Stearns, *The Street I Know*, p. 158.

language of criticism, the old genteel style, was no longer adequate to express the new concepts and new modes of feeling in which the age abounded, he complained that the tyros were not so much incompetent as conventional:

The attempts made to avoid certain *cliches* were almost worse than the *cliches* themselves . . . and when the technique was unfamiliar, they invariably had recourse to broad generalizations, which seldom had any real or genuine applicability to the specific use of this new technique in the book under discussion.[5]

Those who edited intellectual magazines in the early part of the twenties had, then, as these comments suggest, to meet the problem of style in several ways: they had to fight the "new" illiteracy, to destroy the jargon of the old school (if they wanted vivid, intelligent writing), and to take a stand on a kind of journalistic criticism which was struggling to absorb psychoanalysis, the terminology of the new social sciences, and the experiments in creative writing and the plastic arts.

The *Freeman* emerged, under the leadership of Brooks and Nock, with a reputation for brilliant editing and intellectual substance in its reviews of literature and of the other arts and of cultural matters in general. In one of the early numbers Nock had urged contributors to "leaven serious-mindedness with imagination and humour" and to write for the ear; and on these scores of urbanity and euphony both writers, different as they were, could qualify as models.[6] At its most conservative, the *Freeman* reflected the prose of Nock which, although

5. *Ibid.*, p. 158.

6. Nock continued with the charge that the solemnity of most of the articles (especially on political subjects), "the dogged, unrelieved, unrelenting prosecution of the subject in its complete statistical order and entirety" was "really very formidable." And turning from matters of tone to those of style, he demanded: "What has become of the art of writing for the ear" in the tradition of the Bible, William Law, Newman, Huxley, Matthew Arnold, Poe, Howells, and William James? See "Concerning Manuscripts," *The Freeman*, I (April 28, 1920), 151–52.

epigrammatic (often at the expense of nuances of thought), mannered in its wit, and frequently pretentious in tone, was nonetheless striking because of its economy and clarity. At its most advanced, the critical writing in the magazine was akin to that of Brooks, revealing little of the lively colloquialism of Pound, but modern in its complexity, in its figurative expression of a play of mind over new subjects and motives.

Because the point of view of both Brooks and Nock was a delimiting factor in the choice of personnel as well as in style, the *Freeman* neither pushed writers of the aesthetic avant-garde nor found a place for the language of the little magazines. The daring intensity with which E. E. Cummings described the "new" and exciting *Poems* (1920) by T. S. Eliot for readers of the *Dial* would have been out of place in the *Freeman* in any issue of its career:

We like that not any of Poems' *fifty-one* pages fails to impress us with an overwhelming sense of technique. . . . By technique we do mean one thing: the alert hatred of normality which, through the lips of a tactile and cohesive adventure, asserts that nobody in general and some one in particular is incorrigibly and actively alive. This someone is, it would seem, the extremely great artist: or he who prefers above everything and within everything the unique dimension of intensity, which it amuses him to substitute in us for the comforting and comfortable furniture of reality.[7]

The discussion of Eliot's *Poems* in the *Freeman* (written by Louis Untermeyer) is in striking contrast: "For the most part," Untermeyer said,

Eliot cares less for his art than he does for his attitudes. Disdaining the usual poetic cant, he falls into another tradition; he leans towards a kind of versifying which, masquerading under the title of

7. Cummings, "T. S. Eliot," *The Dial*, LXVIII (June, 1920), 783. Marianne Moore's reviews and Pound's "Paris Letters" for the *Dial*, as well as sections of D. H. Lawrence's *Studies in Classic American Literature*, published there, are other notable examples of fresh, direct composition.

"occasional" or "social" verse may be found in many a *Lyra Elegantiarum*. . . . For Eliot's gift is seldom the poet's. His contribution is related to poetry only at rare intervals. His lines, for the most part, are written in a new *genre* or, to be more accurate, in the modernization of a surprisingly old one. They are, primarily, a species of mordant light verse: complex and disillusioned *vers de societe*.[8]

This comment of Untermeyer's is an extreme example of conservative criticism in the Freeman, but it serves to illustrate a point. In the aesthetic group the new literature often stimulated the critical imagination to operate in fundamentally new ways, forcing thought to consider and language to express what was primary and distinct in the creative process. What the critic looked for were the actualities of a writer's experience manifested through his technique, his imaginative truth. In expressing what he saw, the critic often turned to the freshness and extravagance of colloquial speech.

There are, of course, in the period and in the *Freeman*, shades and shades of this critical modernism; but writers consciously made distinctions and offered for debate what was aesthetic and what was intellectual in avant-garde criticism. A letter to the editor of the *Freeman* by William Carlos Williams stated the matter very clearly. The intellectual, according to Williams, implies in his criticism that "art is a spontaneous creation, a by-product of happy conjunctions between emotions, instincts, and environment which *only great periods afford*." [9] This is "art from the outside." In contrast,

the thing which every artist sees without the necessity of demonstration because it is part of his own body, the thing which the philosopher writing about art can never see, is that art is the product of a certain sort of living contact that can be made to live,

8. Louis Untermeyer, "Irony de Luxe," *The Freeman*, I (June 30, 1920), 382.

9. All quotations from Williams's letter are taken from "Letters to the Editors," *The Freeman*, II (Jan. 19, 1921), 449.

even for discussion, in no other way: that the so-called fallow periods are no less possessed in this passionate satisfaction than any other. . . . What is needed . . . is not less discussion about art but more and more—but always by artists.

On the whole, the criticism of the arts in the *Freeman* can, then, be identified with an intellectualism which implied a more philosophical and historical than technical interest and a good deal of rather formal stylistic brilliance. It was in the reviewing of literature that the magazine revealed the greatest variety of attitudes and expression. American culture was still predominantly a literary culture; books received the most attention and were presented in the light of a more complicated, because a richer and more familiar, tradition than were the productions in theater, music, and painting that fell within the purview of the magazine. In its treatment of these nonliterary arts one finds a more obvious cultural bias, a more direct concern with the promotion and explanation of native endeavor to the American people, a greater awareness of relations to Europe.

To find reviewers for music, drama, and the plastic arts, and for a book review section whose coverage was thorough, including, ideally, all those publications in the arts and sciences, in politics, philosophy, and religion which the educated layman might want to read, the *Freeman* drew upon a cross section of liberal intellectual America as well as upon some European contributors. The native writers came primarily from the *Seven Arts* group, the fortnightly *Dial,* and from the liberal journalists who were writing for the *Nation,* the *New Republic* and the supplements of the New York and Chicago dailies.[10] But

10. *The Freeman* took over as steady contributors many of the *Seven Arts* and *Dial* people: Ernest Boyd, Lewis Mumford, Conrad Aiken, Lisle Bell, Harold Stearns, H. B. Fuller, Gerold T. Robinson. (Paul Rosenfeld and Robert Morss Lovett, who were associated with this group, went, respectively, to the new *Dial* and the *New Republic.* Rosenfeld and Lovett each contributed one article to the *Freeman* dur-

they came also from the older generation of muckrakers, from university scholars, and from the younger group of free-lance writers who were mainly attracted to the little magazines. During the first two years of the twenties the *Freeman* was more representative of the entire body of advanced American reviewing than later, when the break between the "social" and the "aesthetic" became marked and writers moved about less freely among the editorial offices of the good magazines. Although the paper had no official European correspondents, reports by foreign critics appeared from time to time, while several American and British émigrés became steady contributors. John Gould Fletcher, an American in London, kept the *Freeman* informed about contemporary English poetry; Padraic and Mary Colum, Llewellyn Powys, and Ernest Boyd, all of whom were living in New York in the early years of the twenties, reviewed both American and European literature. The Scotsman Edwin Muir, an important writer in the magazine after its first year, sent in a number of literary essays and reviews from various European capitals during an extended tour of the Continent. The signatures of distinguished old-world critics, such as Bertrand Russell, Arthur Symons, and Elie Faure, appeared occasionally.

Among the approximately two hundred men and women

ing its lifetime.) Certain well-known critics of Brooks's generation were, of course, busy with their own magazines—the Van Dorens with the *Nation*, Eastman and Dell with the *Liberator*, Mencken with the *Smart Set*. Although the latter's pungency would have been congenial, the *Freeman* was not an outlet for Mencken. He wrote for it (in addition to several communications in the correspondence column) only two pieces: an attack on Woodrow Wilson and a Biblical parody, "The Book of Reuben," on the theme of a husbandman (tenant-farmer), who bought out his landlord at $300 an acre and was soon after "on the chopping block." See "A Mysterious Matter," *The Freeman*, I (May 12, 1920), 200–202, and "The Book of Reuben," *The Freeman*, II (Jan. 5, 1921), 397–98.

who wrote reviews for the *Freeman,* the following did sustained work over a period of time:

Conrad Aiken: poetry; from spring, 1921, to summer, 1922

Newton Arvin: literary and cultural criticism; from spring 1921, to end

Charles Beard: history; from summer, 1921, to summer, 1922

Bernard Iddings Bell: religion; from fall, 1922, to winter, 1923

Lisle Bell: general reviewer, wrote many "Shorter Notices" for the book review section; throughout

Edwin Björkman: general reviewer; from summer, 1920, to fall, 1921

Ralph Block: drama; from fall, 1920, to fall, 1921

Edward Townsend Booth: general reviewer; from fall, 1920, to end

Ernest Boyd: general reviewer; from spring, 1920, to winter, 1922

W. H. Chamberlain: politics; from spring, 1920, to winter, 1923

Mary Colum: fiction; from spring, 1921, to end

Padraic Colum: general reviewer; summer, 1920, intermittently thereafter

John Dos Passos: specialist in Spanish literature, then essayist on Spanish culture; from fall, 1920, to winter, 1922

Walter Prichard Eaton: drama; throughout

Maurice Francis Egan: biography and memoirs; from summer, 1922, to fall, 1923

John Gould Fletcher: poetry throughout, general reviewer of literature after summer, 1923

Henry Blake Fuller: general reviewer of literature; from spring, 1921, to end

Isaac Goldberg: Spanish literature; from fall, 1920, to summer, 1923

R. K. Hack: classics; from winter, 1921, to end

Robert Hillyer: poetry; from fall, 1922, to winter 1924

Howard Mumford Jones: general reviewer of literature; from spring, 1920, to spring, 1923

Horace M. Kallen: philosophy; from spring, 1921, to summer, 1922

Alexander Kaun: Russian literature; from fall, 1920, to winter, 1924

Harold Kellock: politics; from fall, 1920, to end; on the editorial staff after February, 7, 1923

Gertrude Bessie King: philosophy; from winter, 1921, to spring, 1923

R. H. Lowie: anthropology; throughout

John Macy: general reviewer of literature; from winter, 1921, to spring, 1922

Daniel Gregory Mason: chief music reviewer; from summer, 1920, to fall, 1923

Edwin Muir: essays on literature and art, reviews; from winter, 1921, to end

Lewis Mumford: art, literature, and cultural criticism; from summer, 1921, to end.

Walter Pach: chief art reviewer; from summer, 1920, to end

Llewellyn Powys: general reviewer of literature; from fall, 1920, to end

Richard Roberts: religion; from summer, 1920, to summer, 1923

Constance Rourke: general reviewer of literature; from summer, 1920, to fall, 1921

Edward Sapir: anthropology; from spring, 1921, to fall, 1923

Herman George Scheffauer: specialist on the arts in Germany; throughout

Temple Scott: religion; from spring, 1921, to fall, 1923

Herman Simpson: politics; from summer, 1922, to summer, 1923

Harold Stearns: literature and culture criticism; from summer, 1920, to summer, 1922

Henry Logan Stuart: general reviewer; from spring, 1922, to winter, 1924

Joseph L. Tynan: general reviewer; from winter, 1922, to spring, 1923

Louis Untermeyer: poetry, infrequent but important policy-making reviews; from fall, 1920, to spring, 1923

Anne Goodwin Winslow: general reviewer of literature; from spring, 1922, to winter, 1923

Cuthbert Wright: literature and drama; from winter, 1921, to fall, 1923

On the whole the *Freeman* assembled a body of contributors who took a middle position on developments in contemporary letters and the other arts and were often sympathetic to Brooks's social criticism. Reviewers in the special fields of philosophy, history, and the social sciences interpreted their subjects in the light of the same liberal critical consciousness which pervaded the writing on the arts.

The writers of consequence whom the *Freeman* discovered or developed were John Dos Passos, Constance Rourke, Newton Arvin, Edwin Muir, and Lewis Mumford. While it printed pieces by Gorham B. Munson and Kenneth Burke (the founders of *Secession*), Gilbert Seldes, and Malcolm Cowley, these men appeared more frequently in the *Dial*. Edmund Wilson, who became a *New Republic* writer in 1922 and whose reviews combined a cultural sense with literary intelligence in the mode of the very best criticism in the *Freeman*, wrote only two reviews for the magazine.[11]

11. See "The Poetry of Mr. W. B. Yeats," *The Freeman*, V (March 29, 1922), 68–69; and "Mr. Rosenfeld's Musical Chronicle," *The Freeman*, VIII (Feb. 29, 1924), 594–96.

In its treatment of contemporary poetry, fiction, literary and cultural criticism and their tradition, the tone was set by the major reviewers—John Gould Fletcher, Louis Untermeyer, Mary Colum, Newton Arvin, Henry B. Fuller, and Edwin Muir—none of whom, different as they were, was committed to the "mutual benefit and protection societies and magazines devoted to the propaganda of secret writings" toward which Brooks and Nock became increasingly censorious. A reserve about experimentalism characterized a number of the leading critics for the other arts—Lewis Mumford for painting, sculpture, and architecture; Daniel Gregory Mason for music; and Walter Prichard Eaton for drama. Walter Pach, the *Freeman*'s authority on painting and a champion of modern art, was an exception; yet, a cultural emphasis in his writing for the magazine aligns him with the point of view of the other writers. In the reviewing of history, philosophy, and the social sciences no one writer stands out as a policy maker; Charles Beard may be cited, however, as the most distinguished representative of the liberal social consciousness which marked the reviewing in these fields.

Of the reviewers of literature, Fletcher contributed the largest number of essays over the longest period of time, on the average of eleven a year. At first he wrote almost exclusively on British poetry, but later on other genres as well.[12] A

12. Fletcher's first review in the *Freeman*, a favorable discussion of D. H. Lawrence's *New Poems*, appeared in the issue for July 21, 1920. In his autobiography, *Life Is My Song*, he evidently suffers a lapse of memory about his connection with the *Freeman*, for he implies that he first wrote for the magazine in 1923. He recounts how, during a brief five weeks' stay in New York City, he sought out Van Wyck Brooks and offered himself as the English correspondent for the magazine. Brooks told him that, although "his fellow editors were interested in England, both socially and intellectually, the idea of having any correspondents—for anything else but wars, finance and politics—had not yet penetrated their minds." But Brooks promised him, since "no one in the office . . . knew much about poetry," the reviewing of all the

classmate of Brooks at Harvard, a contemporary of Pound and, like him, a pioneer émigré to London, Fletcher was one of the original Imagists and claimed to be the discoverer of the French Symbolists.[13] His poetry was influenced by the Symbolists but also by Whitman; he had been attracted to the social criticism of Brooks, whose *America's Coming-of-Age* and *Letters and Leadership* "seemed . . . to state better and more honestly than any books [he] knew the actual hopes for maturity as well as the moral dilemmas . . . facing America." [14] Fletcher declared himself more at home on the *Freeman* than on Eliot's *Criterion*—in 1923 the only other journal which published his writings—for the disparity between Eliot's classical criticism and his ultraromantic poetry bothered him.[15]

On the subject of contemporary verse Fletcher wrote for readers of the *Freeman* authoritative and discriminating reviews, whose learning and taste often performed the task of weighing the ephemeral reputations of the period that puzzle later readers. He was severe, for example, about Louis Untermeyer's anthology, *Modern British Poetry* (1920), because it devoted eleven pages to Alfred Noyes and only three to Thomas Hardy, and he punctured Vachel Lindsay's European success by maintaining that he was an evangelical Protestant who had "taken" abroad because he was thought to be typically American. Acting as a connoisseur, Fletcher placed Wallace Stevens's poetry in *Harmonium* "head and shoulders above" the best of the Sitwells, Paul Valéry's "Jean Parque," and—provocatively— "The Waste Land." [16] Fletcher's last piece for the *Freeman*

poetry books that came in. Fletcher remembers that he found Brooks, who had been at Harvard the same time as himself but whom he had not known, "a finely balanced, generous, and sensitive son of New England, equally interested in literature from the point of view of the aesthetic as well as the moral point of view." See *Life Is My Song,* pp. 300–301.

13. *Ibid.,* pp. 73–74.     14. *Ibid.,* p. 300.     15. *Ibid.,* p. 301.
16. For reviews of Untermeyer, Lindsay, and Stevens see the follow-

struck the Brooksian note: Robert Frost, unlike most Americans, had managed to live in America without being utterly destroyed, yet because he had not mastered his world as great poets do, his talent was only secondary. His career suggested that:

America for all its recent emergence into the condition of a culture-bearing and art-creating country, is still the land of unfulfilled and creatively starved lives. In Europe one fits into one's environment, or rises superior to it. In America one fits, or reacts against it, or one is crushed.[17]

Modern fiction was interpreted for the *Freeman* primarily by Mary Colum, who had come to America in 1915 from Dublin and the Irish renaissance. After she began to write for the magazine in May, 1921, she contributed articles on D. H. Lawrence, Booth Tarkington, Sherwood Anderson, F. Scott Fitzgerald, Floyd Dell, Waldo Frank, Aldous Huxley, Rebecca West, Willa Cather, Daniel Corkery, Virginia Woolf, and James Joyce. An admirer of Brooks's ideas, Mary Colum dealt more in her reviews with the artist's relation to society than with his technique, and, with Brooks, she took a stand against experimentalism.[18] Stating her position fully in an essay entitled "Where Realism Ends," she defined the two trends in contemporary fiction as regionalism (represented by Sherwood Anderson, Willa Cather, Hardy, and the Irish writers), and a

---

ing issues of the *Freeman*, respectively: "Anthologia Contra Mundum," II (Oct. 13, 1920), 116; "Safe and Sane Romanticism," VIII (Sept. 12, 1923), 22–23; "The Revival of Aestheticism," VIII (Dec. 19, 1923), 355–56.

17. John Gould Fletcher, "The Question of Environment," *The Freeman*, VIII (Feb. 27, 1924), 593–94.

18. Mrs. Colum wrote an enthusiastic appraisal of Brooks in 1924 when many of his fellow critics were attacking him. See "An American Critic: Van Wyck Brooks," *The Dial*, LXXVI (Jan., 1924), 33–41. In her autobiography she called Nock "one of the most discerning and accomplished editors this country has ever seen." See *Life and the Dream*, p. 342.

study of man "in relation to himself and his own subconscious-
ness" (exemplified by Joyce, Proust, and Virginia Woolf).[19]
She preferred regionalism. It had, she wrote, more possibilities
for development, while

the probing into the subconscious has gone about as far as it can
go and still remain in the realm of literature. Men in their sub-
consciousness are too much alike for the study of many subconsciousnesses to remain interesting; it is only in their consciousness
that they become differentiated enough to become varied and interesting.

In any case she warned that the Joycean technique was not for
lesser writers: "most of the efforts that pass for ultramodernism
and which are taken seriously by some of our advanced periodicals are, as far as literature is concerned, sheer drivel."

Mary Colum's critical appreciations of certain modern
writers, especially of Sherwood Anderson and D. H. Lawrence
(the latter was often scorned by pigmy and giant alike), were
large-minded and illuminating. But the sum of her reviews for
the *Freeman* leaves the impression of a diffuse, limited, even
doctrinaire critic. Moral preoccupations get in the way of
judgment, the distrust of the "subconscious" is repetitive, the
failure to reach the heart of a book is too frequent, and, not
sensing the fusion of naturalistic and symbolic strains in modern
psychological fiction, she was unable to write of it with the
depth of understanding possessed by at least a few writers of
the period, notably Edmund Wilson.[20] A European, Mary
Colum's special authority as a *Freeman* critic was the foreign
yardstick by which she measured American writing. Both the
assurance and the fresh responses of the old world observer
were hers, giving weight and flavor, and sometimes condescen-
sion, to her discoveries about our national consciousness.

19. All quotations from the essay are taken from Mary Colum, "Where
Realism Ends," *The Freeman*, VIII (Sept. 26, 1923), 56–58.
20. See the account of her review of *Ulysses*, Chapter VI, pp. 155–56.

The responsibility for many of the *Freeman's* judgments upon recent books of literary criticism lay with Newton Arvin, who was twenty-one and an instructor of English at Smith College when he made his first contribution to the *Freeman* in March, 1921. He wrote often for the paper thereafter, identifying himself with the tradition of Randolph Bourne and the social pessimism of the "young intellectuals." It was Arvin's job to review such key books of the period as Stearns's *America and the Young Intellectual* (where he outdid the author in his disparagement of America), Paul Elmer More's *A New England Group and Others: Shelborne Essays* (described as a critical point of view unfortunately secluded from "real life"), and Stuart P. Sherman's *The Genius in America: Studies in Behalf of the Younger Generation* (the occasion for another account in the *Freeman* of Sherman's failure to understand either the young intellectual or his times).[21] Writing stiffly and pedantically at first, Arvin later used his learning with ease on a wide variety of subjects. His leading review of *Prejudices: Third Series* was an excellent appraisal of H. L. Mencken as an iconoclast, stylist, humorist, and literary dictator in his period.

If Newton Arvin's reviews represented, for their time, a kind of sophisticated academic modernism, those of Henry B. Fuller had about them the high style and urbane wit of the old-fashioned scholarly layman. At the age of sixty-two, having produced his important realistic novels almost twenty years before, Fuller had again come before the public as a contributor

21. See, respectively, the following issues of the *Freeman*: "The Foundering Grandsons," IV (Jan. 18, 1922), 450–51; "The Everlasting No," III (June 1, 1921), 283–84; "Tilting at Windmills," VII (July 11, 1923), 429–30. The *Freeman* was not always against Sherman. Nock had ridiculed him for writing *The Significance of Sinclair Lewis*, but, in Brooks's absence, devoted a "Reviewer's Notebook" to a laudatory review of Sherman's "The Point of View in American Criticism." See *The Freeman*, VI (Nov. 29, 1922), 286–87.

to the intellectual magazines. Beginning to write for the *Freeman* in May, 1921, he commented on a variety of genres, most frequently on biography and historical criticism, and his pieces were nearly always given the first position in the literary section. He wrote, therefore, what the paper considered some of its most important reviews—of Cabell's *Figures of the Earth*, of Strachey's *Queen Victoria*, of Croce's *Dante* (Fuller also contributed an essay on the art of Dante to commemorate the six-hundredth anniversary of his death), of Hamlin Garland's *A Daughter of the Middle Border*, of Preserved Smith's *Erasmus*, of C. G. Coulton's *Chaucer and His England*, of Percy Lubbock's *The Craft of Fiction*.

Fuller's reviews were bravura examples of the *Freeman*'s conservative side in letters. He brought to the magazine three decades of reading and writing experience, from the realism of Howells to the rediscovery of Henry James.[22] He could compose a gracious and sympathetic account of Garland's autobiographies ("most of the [humanities] are becomingly present; you feel them on every page"), even though he had burlesqued Garland in *Under the Skylights* twenty years before.[23] He could censure Cabell mildly for his social irresponsibility in a prose which was ornate, purple, and elegant; half a loving parody of Cabell, half akin to his own elegance.

Shall we not indeed see Mr. Cabell as a prankish priest intent, behind some veil, upon his mystery? Not all cults and their hierophants have invariably worked towards piety, nor under the sense of a keen social and moral responsibility. On the contrary.

22. Fuller had sponsored *Poetry* and contributed to the fortnightly *Dial*. He said in a letter to Brooks: "As a result of recent contributions in the *Freeman*, and elsewhere, I find myself under increasing comment as a novelist at the very time when I have left novel-writing quite behind. So perversely do things go a begging! It won't be so agreeable to be let alone." Quoted in Griffin, *Henry Blake Fuller*, p. 68.

23. Henry B. Fuller, "Three Generations," *The Freeman*, IV (Nov. 9, 1921), 210–11.

Yet we might ask our mystic to descend to the foot of his Tower or to the fore-court of his temple, putting his foot on firm, honest ground, looking about regardfully for the presence of friends and neighbors, and asking himself whether, after all, he hasn't some duty towards them if only the negative duty of being more discreet.

But here we are, demanding the most footless and futile of things —asking an artist to make himself over, to alter the essential hang of his character, and to change the general sweep of his literary draperies. A man's character is like a pair of trousers—tinker with them ever so little, and you alter the whole swing; for better, if you know how; for worse, if you don't. Shall we take the responsibility of altering the *pantalon* under discussion? On the whole, no. Decorum would doubtless gain, but the world would dull, the Flesh would pale, the Devil would droop, and the high horse of Invention would lower his proud crest beyond the certainty of a pick-up.[24]

One could not, in all conscience, Fuller concluded in his review, recommend the wicked Cabell to the young, but for the "experienced and determined adult" who can "follow closely a conscious artist in his work of self-realization," Cabell is a "cate ambrosial."

Fuller's indulgence of artistry as fantasy in the author of *Jurgen* did not extend to a conviction that artistry had rights in fiction in general. Like many other advocates of realism in his day, Fuller considered Cabell outside the rules, as it were. But he drew back in caution and disapproval when a book appeared that declared the artistry of Henry James to be supreme among nineteenth-century novelists. This book was Percy Lubbock's *The Craft of Fiction* (which the aesthetic *Dial* welcomed with joy). Fuller's review in the *Freeman* was at first sardonic: referring to Lubbock's qualifications concerning the craftsmanship of Tolstoy, Flaubert, Dickens, and George Meredith, Fuller asked:

24. All quotations from this review are taken from Henry B. Fuller, "One on a Tower," *The Freeman*, III (May 4, 1921), 186–87.

What Cato is still absent from the forum? . . . The angelic host, soaring above the American expatriates in the bright, clear air of Paris, descends upon Strether and Chad and Maria Gostrey and Mme. de Vionnet, and unveils the mystery. In a word, the climax is Henry James; he is the one far-off, divine event towards which the art of fiction, through several generations, has been tending.[25]

After tracing in ironic vein Lubbock's account of other great novelists' deficiencies, Fuller concluded gently but seriously that Lubbock's full commitment to a method was dangerous, for it might lead the "amateur of the novel" into dehumanizing abstraction.

Fuller's review of *The Craft of Fiction* formed another chapter in the *Freeman's* fear of literary technique, which to Brooks and to so many of its contributors seemed (like the machine) a vise to imprison the creative spirit of man. While the analogy is never actually stated by any one writer, the association between the mechanical properties of technique and, as Lewis Mumford once called it, "the buzzing, screeching, clanking mechanism of modern industrial civilization" is often implicit: both are enemies of the human spirit and threaten the power of its expression to be true and free. Contrast Pound's belief that artists can escape from the mechanism of modern industrial America and its conventional, dishonest art through technique rightly understood ("bad technique is 'bearing false witness' "); or the feeling pervasive in the *Dial* that technique is a living thing, as E. E. Cummings said in his review of Eliot, "the alert hatred of normality which, through the lips of a tactile and cohesive adventure, asserts that nobody in general and someone in particular is incorrigibly and actively alive." The difference marks the *Freeman's* character as an organ of the social criticism and as a magazine of transition. This transition was from a modernism that distrusted the felicities of genteel writing to a

25. Henry B. Fuller, "The Art of Fiction-Writing," *The Freeman*, V (May 3, 1922), 189–90.

modernism in which technique became the key to a piece of writing as an organic whole. It is interesting to observe the variety of ways in which *Freeman* writers refused or approached the jump.

Perhaps the most modern and certainly the most dashing of literary critics in the magazine was Edwin Muir, who presented his readers with a brilliantly generalized psychology and philosophy of art, along with reviews of British and European figures, such as George Douglas, I. A. Bunin, Aldous Huxley, Johann Hölderlin, Knut Hamsun, Hugo von Hofmannsthal, D. H. Lawrence, Nietzsche, Ibsen, Dostoyevsky. The son of a Scotch peasant in the Orkneys, and largely a self-educated man, Muir describes himself as having gone through several stages of development—evangelicism, socialism, Nietzscheanism, psychoanalysis—by his middle thirties, and he was apparently moved by them all when he came to write for the *Freeman* in 1921.[26] After being an editorial assistant on Alfred Orage's *New Age* for two years previous to this time, Muir and his wife had decided "to see Europe and for four years lived in various countries there . . . where [they] were supported mainly by his contributions to the *Freeman* under the generous editorship of Van Wyck Brooks."[27] To Brooks, who reviewed Muir's book of aphorisms, *We Moderns*, in 1920, this Scotsman had seemed a splendid and fearless iconoclast, a daring representative of the contemporary spirit in its battle against the mass fatalism of the age.[28]

26. See the article on Edwin Muir in Kunitz and Haycraft, eds., *Twentieth Century American Authors*.

27. Quoted from Muir's autobiographical note in Kunitz and Haycraft, eds., *Twentieth Century American Authors*. Muir supplements this statement in his *Autobiography* (p. 189). Speaking of his life in Prague, he says: "We had a great deal of leisure, for living was cheap and I could make enough to keep us going by writing two articles a month for the *Freeman* and a weekly article for the *New Age*."

28. Brooks's review concluded: "At a moment when mass fatalism was never more general, when determinism has become not a conviction but

Muir writes in his autobiography (1954) that, looking back over his essays written for the *Freeman* during this time, he was impressed with "how very little" he was concerned with "the truth of what he said," with how he was "simply letting [his] mind range freely among ideas as if that were a sufficient end in itself." [29] But these essays are significant, nonetheless, for what he wrote was a vital expressionistic criticism with which to break the surfaces of conventional reviewing. He defined his position in "A Plea for Psychology in Literary Criticism": [30]

The method of a radical criticism must be psychological. What is it that the psychologist must look for in a work of art? In the first place, the man who expresses himself through it; not, be it observed the man *qua* man, citizen, father of a family, or social figure, but the man as he is, in the old religious phrase, "before God," the man in his relation to reality. . . .

What is the method of this psychology? It is not mysterious; it is the method, on the contrary, which has been used by the greatest critics of all ages. The truths to be discovered, what in a writer is unique (the psychology of man) and what in a writer is universal (the psychology of art), are to be found in the immemorial paths of criticism, in such things as style, subject-matter, conception. True criticism is distinguished from false by this, that while the latter studies these things as ends, talking of style, for instance, as something disembodied, the former sees them in living relation. To the one, the style is good or bad, the treatment true or not true

---

a creed, when 'freedom' is demanded by all and universally misunderstood, such a book is a capital event. It is meat for the strong and wine for the lover of life." See "We Moderns," *The Freeman*, I (May 12, 1920), 214. Commenting on *We Moderns* in his *Autobiography* (p. 151), Muir was glad to say that the book was out of print, for it was full of superficial paradoxes.

29. Muir, *Autobiography*, pp. 199–200.

30. This essay is not printed in the *Freeman*, but appears in a collection of Muir's writing composed largely of pieces originally written for the magazine. The collection, *Latitudes*, was published in New York in 1924 by B. W. Huebsch and is one of several books which grew out of the *Freeman's* writers' work for the magazine: Lewis Mumford's *Sticks and Stones*, Walter Pach's *The Masters of Modern Art*, Stearns's *America and the Young Intellectual*. See *Latitudes*, pp. 97–100.

to life; to the other, style and treatment are in addition symbols, or, more exactly, symptoms. This method is very fruitful. We learn much about Mr. Hardy, for instance, when we discover on analyzing his characters that they are without will and that for their author the dynamic principle exists in the outer world only. An analysis of "Ghosts" would be just as illuminating; it would reveal within Ibsen an optimistic reformer confronted continually by a tragic poet.[31]

Such things needed to be said in 1922. Using this method, Muir, in his reviews for the *Freeman*, especially of the great nineteenth-century moderns—Dostoyevsky, Ibsen, Nietzsche—wrote with more depth, perception, and control, and with more sophistication in his use of psychology, than did any other contributor to the magazine. His was one of the sharpest points of sunlight in the checkered shade of the *Freeman's* garden of contemporary literature.

To turn from the chief reviewers of literature to the chief reviewers of the other arts, one notices that, with the exception of Lewis Mumford, who was twenty-five when he came to the *Freeman*, these men were established critics of the previous decade who had, in one way or another, become interested in furthering an artistic renaissance in America. Walter Prichard Eaton, of the Harvard Class of 1900, had written several books on the American stage and had been the drama critic for two years on the New York *Sun;* he was a voluminous free-lance writer and an apologist for the little theater movement at its inception. Walter Pach had graduated from City College in 1903. By 1920 he had exhibited his paintings in Paris and had become an active art critic; in addition, he had done much to help organize exhibits of modern art in America, notably the Armory Show of 1913 and the series of Independents, which afforded unknown American painters an opportunity to come before the public. Daniel Gregory Mason was a classmate of

31. Muir, *Latitudes*, pp. 97, 99.

Edwin Arlington Robinson's at Harvard in 1895 and had known William Vaughan Moody and Edward MacDowell. A contributor on musical subjects to New York magazines for twenty years, a teacher at Columbia University, and a composer, Mason came to think that Brooks's "Notebooks" in the *Freeman* painted a picture of American letters which had its counterpart in music, for, he wrote in his autobiography, "we were trying . . . to develop a sense of fellowship in art as a protection against the chaos by which we were surrounded." [32] The "young intellectual," Lewis Mumford, had left Stuyvesant High School in New York in 1912 to be a writer. He became a few years later a disciple of Sir Patrick Geddes, worked as an inspector in the garment industry, served in the navy for a year in 1918, and then joined the editorial staff of the older *Dial* for a brief time in 1919. When the *Freeman* began publication in March, 1920, Mumford was acting as a visiting editor of the *Sociological Review* in London.

Writing largely of productions, concerts, festivals, exhibits, and buildings, these chief critics conveyed a tangible sense of an audience which must be saved from the debilitating intellectual poverty of American life. The problems of creating a rapport between this audience and the artist and of finding a usable tradition for both were constantly brought before the reader.

Neither an exciting nor intransigent critic, Mason filled the role of a popularizer of musical knowledge and taste, reinforcing unequivocally the *Freeman's* essential antipathy to experimentalism in the arts. In two articles addressed to "the plain man," he deplored the decadence of "our professional music," advancing as the most striking symptoms of this decadence "the almost universal preoccupation with manner at the expense of matter" and the snobbery of the accepted organs of ultra modernism, such as the *Dial* in America, the *Ches-*

32. Mason, *Music in My Time*, p. 395.

*terian* in England, the *Revue Musicale* in France, which prefer Stravinsky, Scriabin, Schönberg, Prokofiev, Satie, and Arthur Bliss to such great composers as Brahms, Schubert, Verdi, César Franck, Moussorgsky—and to Elgar, Richard Strauss, and Vincent d'Indy.[33] The latter are those to whom the "plain man," transcending national or coterie boundaries, is instinctively drawn. Between the "plain man" and the "high-brows," Mason explained, are the "Philistines," who like jazz and fill boxes at the opera. As a means of advancing music throughout the country, Mason advocated the establishment of glee clubs and college orchestras as a better form of education and enjoyment than listening to recordings.[34] He shared with Albert Jay Nock and other editors of the *Freeman* a belief that there were signs of a popular revival of music in America. Their prophecy was a sound one, even if they failed to foresee the importance of recordings and the dignity of jazz in its fulfillment.

In addition to his analyses of current taste, Mason wrote for the *Freeman* appreciations of d'Indy and Vaughan Williams, reported on the Pittsfield Music Festival, described the styles of contemporary music in Germany and Italy, and reviewed books on musical literature. Mason's pieces made up a large body of the *Freeman's* music criticism. His work was supplemented by formal and incidental comments from three of the editors who were particularly interested in music, Nock, Neilson, and Huebsch, and by single contributions from such men as Jerome Hart, who described the conductors of the 1920 season, Ernest Brennecke, who wrote on Erik Satie, B. H. Haggin, who attacked as sentimental any appreciation of music which did not involve an understanding of its technique, and

33. Daniel Gregory Mason, "The Plain Man and Music," *The Freeman*, VII (July 4, 1923), 399–400.
34. Daniel Gregory Mason, "Music and the Plain Man," *The Freeman*, VII (June 13, 1923), 327–29.

Henry Cowell and Robert L. Duffus, who presented in three essays a history of harmonic development.

Walter Pach stands out as an advanced critic on art for the *Freeman*. Possessed of balance and good taste, he was open-minded toward all forms of modernism, including the cubists. The main themes of his cultural avant-gardism in the *Freeman* were the possibilities for developing a native tradition in painting, the relation of American art to European, especially to the work of the French Impressionists and their successors, and the whole problem of "Art in America" (to quote the title of a series of articles Pach wrote for the magazine in the winter of 1920). Pach believed that America had had no great painters except for Albert Pinkham Ryder, but that there were signs of hope for the future in the work of a few young native artists.[35] These could learn much from Europe, Pach declared, for it is impossible to determine if native or foreign ideas prevail in a culture.[36] At present the best art in America was functional—her bridges, her machines, her architecture.[37] On the whole, we were an underprivileged country as far as artists and their audience were concerned. There was small interest in the country at large in painting and the plastic arts, the greater part of the population had had almost no opportunity to see the great works of the past, and there were few buyers for the work of Americans. The latter situation suggested government subsidy as a remedy, but this could prove very dangerous. Only the great genius of French art had saved it from the corrupting effect of government aid. In America, where the springs of inspiration were so much weaker, bureaucratic patronage might foster something very base indeed.

35. Walter Pach, "Art in America" II, *The Freeman*, II (Nov. 17, 1920), 232.

36. Walter Pach, "Paris in New York," *The Freeman*, II (Feb. 2, 1921), 492.

37. Walter Pach, "Art in America," II, *The Freeman*, II (Nov. 17, 1920), 232.

Pach speculated that in the future, as Clive Bell has suggested, some plan might be evolved whereby "any person wishing to be an artist [might] be given a bare living from the public funds; the idea being that the meagerness of such a life would prove unattractive to the mere idler." [38] Such an experiment in America seemed extremely unlikely; yet, Pach concluded with Utopian gusto:

[The] plan has all the savor of that better time one cannot help dreaming of, when the lust for possession, which must surely be approaching its climax in this epoch, will be displaced by an ideal of achievement in the intellectual domain. The ghoulish ugliness of the work of governments and men in this *post bellum* period makes that better time seem far off indeed; but though the spirit that makes for the right standard of values is slow and weak today, it is a deathless spirit and we can not say the hour or the day when it is ready to receive a mighty access of force, a power that will enable it to sweep through all the mass of mankind.[39]

Pach's treatment of modernism in painting for the *Freeman* was thorough, for the paper published in 1923 as a series of eight articles the chapters which made up his *The Masters of Modern Art.*

In Walter Prichard Eaton's reviewing of the theater, the issues of freedom for the artist and of training an appreciative audience were also paramount. In this case the threat was, naturally, commerical Broadway; the hope for the future lay in the Provincetown Players and other such amateur groups, or, for professionals, in the Theater Guild, or in a drama league, which, in contrast to a concern with art plays belonging to the little theater, would promote throughout the country the production of any kind of drama that could keep the theatrical instinct alive. Toward current plays and experimental theories of stagecraft, Eaton's attitude was, relatively speaking, con-

38. Walter Pach, "Art in America," Part I, *The Freeman*, II (Nov. 10, 1920), 207.
39. *Ibid.*, p. 207.

servative. On the whole issue of expressionism, raised by the work of Robert Edmund Jones and by Kenneth MacGowan's *The Theatre of Tomorrow*, Eaton, speaking officially for the *Freeman*, was cautious, because he believed that the native dramatic genius of America was essentially realistic, that realism in the American theater had never been given a fair chance, and that realism afforded the American drama the greatest opportunity to comment seriously upon life. "Creative realism," with its potentialities for "a more profound and searching emotionalism . . . without sacrifice of the social criticism, the intellectual values of the best modern drama," must be fully tried, he maintained, "though [this realism] will sacrifice . . . some of the more far-reaching aspirations of the theatre-painters." [40] Eugene O'Neill, who had given the *Freeman* a chance to comment on four powerful plays, *Lost Horizon*, *Anna Christie*, *The Emperor Jones*, *The Hairy Ape*, was, however, praised highly by Eaton in both his naturalistic and expressionistic phases.

Against the rock of Eaton's dramatic criticism and reviewing, the convictions of other writers on the theater splashed up now and then a wave of protest. For example, Kenneth MacGowan maintained in a defense of expressionism that

the dramatist's special business [is] to master the extremely difficult task of fighting through to Form while retaining the realistic technique, or else—which seems far better—frankly to desert realism, representation, illusion, and write directly in significant terms, no matter how unplausible they may be.[41]

Louis Baury, in contrast to Eaton's panegyric on *The Hairy Ape* (which for him had transcended the drama of realism or "poetic suggestion" to something splendid and entirely new),

40. Walter Prichard Eaton, "The Theatre of Tomorrow," *The Freeman*, V (May 10, 1922), 214.

41. Kenneth MacGowan, "The Living Stage," *The Freeman*, VI (Nov. 1, 1922), 185.

said that O'Neill had failed to achieve in this play any "real fusion of the underlying idea with the method of presentation; which is to say, there is no drama." [42]

Lying within the purview of both "theatre" and "art" was "the motion-picture," as the *Freeman* usually called it, a form less than a generation old and capable of arousing strong hopes and fears. Eaton was decidedly a skeptic. He maintained that the movies were a threat to serious drama, not as a potentially comparable art form, but because producers and playwrights were being bought by a growing industry that offered large profits and a large undiscriminating audience. As to the artistic properties of the motion-picture, "individuality on the screen was impossible"; Eaton called this medium, in a review of *Kismet,* a "harsh, unlovely square of light [where] photographs were bobbing about in dumb show, cold and colorless." [43] Several other writers for the *Freeman,* however, saw the new form as a potentially great one. Ralph Block asserted that its future lay in being a vehicle for naturalism (in contrast to Charlie Chaplin's exploitation of the cinema's pantomimic properties) by working for "a more exact and more appropriate selection of gesture" and a "more closely woven texture of representation." [44] *Dr. Caligari* was offered by Herman George Scheffauer as a magnificent example of what the movies could do to create a world of "intense relief and depth . . . a stereoscopic universe"; for him their future lay in "the vivifying of space." [45] But the height of faith was reached by Elie Faure, who affirmed in "The Art of Cineplastics" that the

42. See, respectively, Walter Prichard Eaton, "The Hairy Ape," *The Freeman,* V (April 26, 1922), 160; and Louis Baury, "Mr. O'Neill's New Plays," *The Freeman,* V (May 3, 1922), 185.

43. Walter Prichard Eaton, "A Skeptic At the Movies," *The Freeman,* II (Dec. 15, 1920), 329.

44. Ralph Block, "Pantomine," *The Freeman,* I (Sept. 1, 1920), 592–93.

45. Herman George Scheffauer, "The Vivifying of Space," *The Freeman,* II (Nov. 24, 1920), 249.

motion-picture was essentially American in character, "primitive" and "barbarous" like Americans,

among whom the cinema . . . will assume its full significance as plastic drama in action, occupying time through its own movement and carrying with it its own space, of a kind that places it, balances it and gives it the social and psychological value it has for us.[46]

This new fully developed art form will be suited, Faure declared, to the new "form of plastic civilization" for which men are seeking, a civilization "that is undoubtedly destined to substitute for analytic states and crises of the soul, synthetic poems of masses and great ensembles in action." [47]

Faure's generalizations represent a kind of theorizing about the inter-relationships of art and culture, which often provided exciting material in the *Freeman* and which gave expression to its modernism in contrast to the manner, if not the intent, of the treatments of society by the older generation. Lewis Mumford, who was in and out of every department, frequently wrote stimulating pieces in this newer, organic vein, especially in his essays on architecture. Working in sympathy with the cultural assumptions of Brooks, Mumford, like his colleagues in the nonliterary arts, focused on the problem of the artist and his audience, making it, indeed, the center of his whole theoretical structure. For his was a cultural avant-gardism based on the need to show men the possibilities of "transforming the instrumentalities of life," as he put it in a controversial article called "Beauty and the Picturesque." [48] Beauty Mumford associated with use; the picturesque with contemplation. The first was "civi-centric," "objective," and "disciplined to the

46. Elie Faure, "The Art of Cineplastics," Part IV, *The Freeman*, III (Aug. 31, 1921), 585.
47. Elie Faure, "The Art of Cineplastics," Part V, *The Freeman*, III (Sept. 7, 1921), 610.
48. Lewis Mumford, "Beauty and the Picturesque," *The Freeman*, III (July 13, 1921), 420.

necessities of the outside world"; the second was "subjective" and "indifferent." [49] To distinguish between them, Mumford maintained, was "essential . . . to an understanding of the place of the arts, and the artist, in the modern world," for

as the picturesque has developed in art, beauty has tended to disappear from life. . . . Whilst the "cultivated few" have become alive to more exquisite aesthetic sensations than their ancestors had probably ever experienced, the "mutilated many" have been forced to live in great cities and abject country towns of a bleakness and ugliness such as the world, if we are to judge by the records that exist, has never known before.[50]

It was the quest for beauty, not the searching of art galleries for the picturesque, Mumford implied (his tone backing the theory), that was of the more worth to society and the higher aim of man, for "the quest for beauty . . . gathers itself into an effort to make finer people, nobler buildings, better ordered theatres of activity." [51] The series of essays on American architecture, which formed the basis of his first book on the subject, *Sticks and Stones* (1924),[52] constituted an exploration of his concept of beauty for his *Freeman* readers. His work for the magazine as a whole supported the philosophy of organicism which he expressed in an early piece, "Towards a Humanist Synthesis," in which he urged, for the preservation of the integrity of man and society, a meeting of the arts and sciences:

All the great humanists, from Confucius to Tolstoy, have sought to lay the foundations of a New Jerusalem. Science cannot remain indifferent to that aim without forfeiting its claim to human respect; for in the end, man is the measure of all things, including

49. Lewis Mumford, "Beauty and the Picturesque," in "Letters to the Editors," *The Freeman*, IV (Sept. 14, 1921), 17.

50. Lewis Mumford, "Beauty and the Picturesque," *The Freeman*, III (July 13, 1921), 420.

51. *Ibid.*, p. 420.

52. Mumford stated in the acknowledgments to this book that "it would not have been put together but for the persistent encouragement and kindly interest of Mr. Albert Jay Nock."

the corpus of knowledge which the scientists have created. When the scientist becomes passionately interested in human life, the social sciences will lie beneath the foundations of the New Jerusalem precisely in the fashion that the physical sciences now underlie the stony exterior of New York.[53]

Mumford expressed in sweeping terms a characteristic concern for man which, in one way or another, animated the corps of reviewers whom the *Freeman* assembled to "command comprehensively, adequately for America, the whole field of human expression." Among them, despite the doubts and fears of the period, the glimmer of a New Jerusalem was rarely absent.

53. Lewis Mumford, "Towards a Humanist Synthesis," *The Freeman*, II (March 2, 1921), 585.

## Chapter Six
# Books for Review

The *Freeman's* choice of books for review during its four years of publication was similar to that of the *Nation*, the *New Republic*, and the *Dial* in those that were judged to be of significance to literary history. While this significance was sometimes indicated indirectly in the *Freeman* by the amount of space the reviewer took to condemn his subject, there is no doubt of the paper's grasp of the vitality and challenge of the current literary life. The *Freeman* gave serious attention, for example, to the fiction of Sherwood Anderson, Sinclair Lewis, F. Scott Fitzgerald, Waldo Frank, and Floyd Dell; to the great European moderns—Lawrence, Joyce, Proust, and Virginia Woolf; to the poetry of Robert Frost, Conrad Aiken, Wallace Stevens, T. S. Eliot, and E. E. Cummings; to the reminiscences, collected letters, biographies, and new editions which revived the memories of James Russell Lowell, Henry and William James, of Melville and Whitman, of Dante, Milton, Keats, Shelley, Matthew Arnold, Tolstoy, Chekhov, Dostoyevsky, Baudelaire, and Nietzsche; in the field of philosophy and intellectual history to John Dewey's *Reconstruction in Philosophy*, Santayana's *Character and Opinion in the United States*, Freud's *Introduction to Psychoanalysis* (reviewed for its cultural and literary implications), Havelock Ellis's *The Dance of Life*, and James Harvey Robinson's *The Mind in the Making*; to such literary sensations of the hour as H. G. Wells's *The Outline of History*, Hendrik Wilhelm Van Loon's *The Story of Mankind*, and Lytton Strachey's *Queen Victoria*; to books of literary criticism such as T. S. Eliot's *The Sacred Wood*, Percy Lubbock's *The Craft of Fiction*, and D. H. Lawrence's *Studies in Classic American Literature*.

Like the two liberal journals of opinion, the *Freeman* devoted considerable space to topical publications "exposing" the war and the peace, of which John Maynard Keynes's *Economic Consequences of the Peace* was the most notable, to accounts and evaluations of "the Russian experiment," and to books which tested in one way or another the liberal's attitude towards capitalistic institutions: *The Americanization of Edward Bok, The Autobiography of Andrew Carnegie,* and Upton Sinclair's *The Brass Check.* While all three magazines covered scholarly works in the fields of sociology and political science, the *Freeman* printed more reviews of such material than did the others.

More consciously European in orientation than the liberal weeklies, the *Freeman* and the *Dial* found different kinds of inspiration and tradition on the Continent. The *Freeman's* sympathies lay with the realist and expressionist movements abroad rather than with the experimentalism which most attracted the *Dial.* And, if the latter thought to find the key to civilization in the figures of *Axel's Castle,* the *Freeman* thought to find it in Russia, in the Scandinavian naturalists— Martin Andersen Nexo and Johan Bojer, in the work of Jules Romains and Anatole France, and in the great nineteenth-century humanists whom Brooks so much admired. As compared with the other advanced magazines in 1920, the *Freeman* began by standing somewhere between the more sophisticated cosmopolitanism of the *Dial* and the simpler nativism of the *New Republic* under Francis Hackett.

In that first year of the decade, when, for its wealth of spirit in politics and the arts, the new magazine was fortunate to be born, the central questions for letters were the evaluation of an active native literature,[1] the re-examination of older writers in the light of the new national consciousness, the exploration of

---

1. Edith Wharton's *Age of Innocence;* Willa Cather's *Youth and the Bright Medusa;* Sherwood Anderson's *Poor White;* Sinclair Lewis's *Main Street;* Floyd Dell's *Moon Calf;* F. Scott Fitzgerald's *This Side*

Freudian psychology for the uses of literary criticism, "the strange experiments in the *Dial* and the *Little Review*" (as Brooks described "aesthetic " writing in 1920), and the establishment of connections with European literature. Underlying all these was the question of the nature of American democracy, its cultural opportunities, and its limitations. As in Brooks's essays, so in the *Freeman's* treatment of books, indeed in its whole presentation of the arts, the cognizance of juxtaposed values was pervasive. America and Europe, old and young, convention and revolt, principle and expediency, highbrow and low-brow, industrial society and the artist, form and content—in this inclination to generalize on a few simple opposites were the nascent ironies of modern criticism.

Brooks's belief in the possibilities of Freudian psychology for the illumination of art and society was also held by other writers. J. D. Beresford wrote, for example, that psychoanalysis "gave a new mystery to the human mind; adumbrated the suggestion of a freer morality by dwelling on the psychical and spiritual necessity for the liberation of impulses; and . . . provided material for comparatively unworked complications of motive." [2] He attempted to explain away the popular notion

---

of *Paradise;* Edna St. Vincent Millay's *A Few Figs from Thistles;* E. A. Robinson's *Lancelot;* T. S. Eliot's *Poems;* Randolph Bourne's *Untimely Papers* and *History of a Literary Radical;* H. L. Mencken's *Prejudices: Second Series;* Ezra Pound's *Instigations;* Eliot's *The Sacred Wood;* and Brooks's *The Ordeal of Mark Twain;* the letters of Henry and William James; George Santayana's *Character and Opinion in the United States.* All of these books were reviewed by the *Freeman* in 1920, except Fitzgerald's novel, Edna Millay's poems, Bourne's *History,* and Brooks's biography. *This Side of Paradise,* published in the spring of 1920, did not come into its own in the *Freeman* until two years later in a review of *The Beautiful and Damned.* Parts of the *Ordeal* were published in the *Freeman,* but the magazine did not review books by its editors; Brooks had also written a preface to Bourne's *History of a Literary Radical.*

2. All quotations from this essay are taken from J. D. Beresford, "Psychoanalysis and the Novel," *The Freeman,* I (March 24, 1920), 35–39.

that the unconscious is the "beast of desire" by a discussion of psychoanalytic theory which concluded with the statement that "it is the shadowed self [the unconscious] that is responsible for what is best and most permanent in our literature." These remarks and the glossing of such terms as "the unconscious," "sub-conscious," and "trauma" suggest the pioneering quality of Freudianism in the first year of the magazine. By 1920, as Frederick Hoffman has said, "the practice and mispractice of psychoanalysis has been the means of spreading the language of the new psychology until it was fairly well misunderstood." [3] The *Freeman*, while it attacked popular misconceptions, sometimes committed errors of its own.

Many of the new paper's critical attitudes established in 1920 remained the same throughout its life. Certainly the first two years, up through 1921, showed a clear continuity in tone. After this time the change in the intellectual temper of the period, the feeling that the energy of revolt per se had spun itself out and must be replaced by aesthetic disciplines and new literary interests, was manifested in the *Freeman*. As we have seen, this change had a negative result in Brooks, who became more distrustful of literary experimentalism as it gained power among artists and intellectuals. His feelings were often seconded by the reviewers. At the same time strength developed in other aspects of reviewing in the *Freeman*: the use of Freudian tools became more assured (for example, the essays of Edwin Muir), and the magazine offered a dazzling array of comments on nineteenth-century European literature to balance American concerns.

Reviews of two books of criticism which the *Freeman* featured, a volume of James Russell Lowell's posthumously published essays and T. S. Eliot's *The Sacred Wood*, bounded the paper's critical territory in 1920, when it was still important to stress the break with the genteel tradition and when the feeling

3. Hoffman, *Freudianism and the Literary Mind*, p. 63.

about the Pound-Eliot group was still open-minded. Van Wyck Brooks wrote the comment on Lowell's *The Function of the Critic and Other Essays* (edited by Albert Mordell):

[This publication] reminds us in a rather startling way that the reputation of our old literary worthies has ceased to be a vested interest and has passed into the hands of the skeptical and irreverent young. . . . This volume . . . is edited by the author of a book as remote as possible from the true Brahminian line, a book the very title of which, "The Erotic Motive in Literature," would have been abhorrent to the Boston of even thirty years ago. Lowell at the mercy of a Freudian and with the sanction of Messers. Houghton and Mifflin! Times have changed indeed! And times have changed when a Riverside preface urges that the reader of Sandburg and Masters may without inconsistency enjoy Longfellow and Whittier *also*.[4]

But it turns out that Lowell's Freudian editor has been merciful; he has not obtruded "an heretical point of view." Rather he has brought together a number of uncollected essays which reveal Lowell "at his best." The volume, therefore, calls for an evaluation of genteel criticism in the hands of so distinguished a critical mind as Lowell's. How "very different" might the present have been, wrote Brooks, in probing this mind, "if, during the last half-century," some one as good as Lowell "had been bent upon shaping a literature in the United States." Unfortunately he "was not the friend of the creative spirit of America whenever it assumed characteristic, that is to say, non-English, non-traditional forms." And he followed "familar grooves" instead of probing the culture of his "own time and place" to reinterpret "the values, as distinguished from the phenomena, of literature." He cannot feed the present generation, which "expects from literature the very bread of life." But one can be nostalgic for the older culture: "[Lowell] has

4. All quotations from this review are taken from "Lowell at His Best," *The Freeman*, I (June 23, 1920), 357–58.

the judgment we gladly dispense with and the verbal felicity we despise, for the lack of which the future will despise and dispense with most of us."

Presented with that seminal work of a new criticism, T. S. Eliot's *The Sacred Wood*, the *Freeman* responded to the power of a critical point of view that, even in 1920, seemed to be needed as another kind of "bread of life." "His book is severe and analytic, and one can think of no two qualities in criticism which are at the moment more desirable," wrote the reviewer, Conrad Aiken.[5] And he praised Eliot equally for his insistence on "the value of tradition" and "on the elimination, as far as possible, of irrelevant emotional factors which may interfere with the best judgment of art. . . . For there is no country," Aiken wrote, "where that doctrine is needed as America needs it." Unusual in the *Freeman's* treatment of Pound and Eliot, this essay makes an identification through style as well as attitude with its subject. Yet, Aiken's praise is not unqualified. He takes Eliot to task for his failure to practice "scientific criticism" by pointing out carefully, first, the inexactness of Eliot's psychological language (his mixing of the terms of Freud, James-Lange, and Remy de Gourmont), then, the fallacy of an aesthetic criticism which works on a secondary plane because it divorces art from society:

It is useless, or nearly useless, to attempt an estimate of the "skill" of a work of art, because, as long as we do not know what the work of art is for, we can not hope to know precisely what will constitute skill. If criticism is to be a science, then we must begin with an attempt to understand what is the function of art, socially and psychologically. . . . This must be the starting-point, and the inquiry will deal very largely, at the outset, precisely with the question of "theme" as distinguishable from "arrangement."

But, in the end, Aiken admits to Eliot's provocativeness:

5. All quotations from this review are taken from Conrad Aiken, "The Scientific Critic," *The Freeman*, II (March 2, 1921), 593–94.

It is a testimonial to the range and ingenuity of [Eliot's] mind that as one puts down his book one thinks of so many points about which one would like to quarrel with him, and quarrel, moreover, respectfully. *Is* "Hamlet" a failure as a work of art? *Does* Mr. Eliot find, in his essay on that play, the "objective correlative" of his conviction? . . . With questions like these Mr. Eliot invites us to a meditation prolonged and delicious.

The core of the *Freeman's* response to literature in the first two years of the decade, however, was neither the expression of revolt in terms of qualified approval of an eminent, genteel critic nor the possibilities of an aestheticism based on the psychology of art and society, but rather an intellectual and emotional interest in the writing which lay close to the changing moral and social structure of America—in the literature of the small town, in the culture figures of the past, and in critiques of American life. In that which, in short, was most sympathetic to the social criticism of the awakening.

The novel of the small town, the "new realism," as Alfred Kazin calls it, had struck home among readers and critics generally because, in giving imaginative structure to what a number of young provincials had actually experienced in the Middle West, it also symbolized the insurrection against the whole genteel and commercial American province which characterized the ambivalent nativism of advanced opinion in 1920. "The new pioneer in this country," said the *New Republic* in an editorial entitled "Main Street in Fiction,"

is the man or woman who  . . . brings provincial experience into aesthetic and spiritual and above all critical consciousness. . . . [America's] present critical acceptance of its own existence is its greatest triumph of social imagination. It is the beginning of one kind of national fullness and integrity, and this is the work of the novelists who have Main Street in hand.[6]

6. "Main Street in Fiction," *The New Republic*, XXV (Jan. 12, 1921), 184.

And the *Nation,* in an unsigned review of Sinclair Lewis's novel and Sherwood Anderson's *Poor White,* spoke of the "iron authenticity" of these writers of the Middle West, "these lovers of beauty once caged in insupportable hideousness," who bring to their readers "the acute vision of their oppressed and distorted youth." [7] Taking a different line, the *Freeman's* review of *Main Street,* written by Herbert Seligman, voiced the theme of European versus American values:

The qualities he [Lewis] opposes to the dullness and religiosity of Gopher Prairie with its Main Street are European; they are the gaiety that springs from the cultivation of imaginative values, tolerance, daring, sensitiveness to human beings and their desires— qualities of living which are not to be expected in their fullness in an American small town, which are not capable of being cultivated in a civilization raw with dollar-seeking.[8]

Only the *Dial* relegated *Main Street* to "Briefer Mention." "The book," it wrote, "has more social than artistic implications, but it is no wonder, for the author has dug his hands in the richest soil in America, and his fingers are a little grubby." [9]

A distinction (suggested by the *Dial*) between the social and artistic implications of the new realism was neglected in the first burst of appreciation in the other magazines. Nor did the *Freeman* make any attempt to relate the new novelists to the work of older realists who published books in 1920. Novels by William Dean Howells,[10] Henry B. Fuller, and Edith Wharton

7. "The Epic of Dullness," *The Nation,* CXI (Nov. 10, 1920), 536.
8. Herbert J. Seligman, "The Tragi-comedy of Main Street," *The Freeman,* II (Nov. 17, 1920), 237.
9. "Briefer Mention," *The Dial,* LXX (Jan., 1921), 106.
10. Howells's *Vacation of the Kelwyns* was published posthumously in 1920. His death that same year was the occasion for an editorial in the *Freeman,* which, without reference to his career as a reformer, fixed his place as that of a novelist of namby-pamby Victorian manners. "The interest attaching to his work," said Albert Jay Nock, "is only such as is communicated to it by a rich and delightful imagination, an unfailing humor, an unfailing dignity and sweetness of temper, and a clear, re-

were presented in "Shorter Notices," with deference, yes, but with no obligation to review their careers or to see them in the light of modern times. It was as if the social truth of Lewis, Dell, and Anderson had sprung, a newborn but fully armed Athena, out of the monstrous head of America. But questions soon followed, in all the magazines, about the artistic properties of the new genre as well as about the validity with which it represented America.

Considering the vogue of the novel of revolt from the viewpoint of classical realism, Albert Jay Nock registered strong protest against the hasty assumptions of many contemporary critics that timely social criticism and good literature were synonymous. He offered Gogol's "Old Fashioned Farmers" as a model to the "younger and more promising story-writers who have chosen to deal with certain phases of American life. . . . Mr. Sinclair Lewis, Mr. Floyd Dell, Mr. Sherwood Anderson, and Mr. Waldo Frank," of whom the reviewers say "they have genius." [11] After attacking these writers' passion for unselected

---

sourceful style. To have carried one's work by the sheer force of these . . . is an immense and praiseworthy achievement . . . and the chances are that the future will marvel at his having fashioned so much that is lovely out of the unloveliness of the pallid and tepid world that remained, for some reason, the world of his permanent choice." See "Mr. Howells's World," *The Freeman*, I (May 26, 1910), 248. Howard Mumford Jones, writing a review of a critical study of Howells in 1923, denied him the position of a realist at all, relegating him to the company of Thackeray and Victorian romanticism. See "A Study of Howells," *The Freeman*, VII (April 25, 1923), 163. Brooks, not surprisingly, added Howells to his list of post-Civil-War failures: "Was Mr. Howells . . . honest, artistically speaking, when to arrive at the doctrine that 'the more smiling aspects of life are the more American,' he deliberately . . . averted his eyes from the darker side of life?" See "A Question of Honesty," *The Freeman*, II, (Feb. 2, 1921) 487. Nowhere in the *Freeman* was the author of *A Traveller from Altruria* and *A Hazard of New Fortunes* accorded an honorable place in the middle-class radical tradition.

11. All quotations from this essay are taken from Albert Jay Nock, "A Study in Literary Temper," *The Freeman*, II (Jan. 26, 1921), 464–67.

documentation, Nock described Gogol's novel as having the qualities of "disinterestedness, tenderness, serenity" which young American writers should "emulate." [12]

An answer to Nock's remarks by Lewis Mumford, appearing in the "Letters to the Editors," was a defense of the modern temper (neither disinterested, nor tender, nor serene) and one of the baldest statements in the magazine of the social critic's "artistic" position. After granting the fact that Lewis, Anderson, Frank, and Dell lacked the classical qualities admired by Nock, Mumford declared:

the literary temper of our generation will never be much improved until our social distemper is to some degree corrected. . . . In the modern novel, human characters dwindle in size; human motives weaken in intensity; human experience loses its sharp significance —between the novelist and his materials has arisen the buzzing, screeching, clanking mechanism called modern industrial civilization. . . . The core of life has been lost within the shell that has developed to protect it, and the writer cannot touch the first element as an artist until somehow he has managed to break his way through the second element as a sociologist.[13]

Mumford's imagery is a vivid reminder of the archetypal metaphor in which American social criticism conceived of the

12. Paul Rosenfeld wrote bitingly in *Men Seen* of "Mr. Nock" and his critical pronouncements in the *Freeman:* "We ought to be jubilant, we in America who are in need of learning. It appears that we are about to be taught. There is someone who says he can procure us 'sound spiritual guidance.' We are also to be given the opportunity of becoming great artists. For the sound spiritual guides are going to 'set before us the great examples of classic work' to 'stimulate our feelings for great classic work' and give us 'assurance that the effect of this great classic work can be reproduced and assist us in reproducing it.'" By his own words, Rosenfeld continued, "he demonstrates that he has neither an understanding of the creative nor the critical processes, if two indeed they are. For he implies that creation is an attempt to reproduce the effect of other works, and that the function of criticism is to assure the creator that reproductions can be made and to assist him in making them." See "Mr. Nock," in *Men Seen*, pp. 325, 341.

13. Lewis Mumford, "A Study in Social Distemper," in "Letters to the Editors," *The Freeman*, II (Feb. 9, 1921), 519–20.

creative spirit as imprisoned by the machine. The intensity of his writing re-emphasizes for us the single-mindedness of this criticism, the blinders that "breaking through as a sociologist" could put on the faculties of its practitioners. A fuller vision was not lacking, however, even among those more in sympathy with the sociological and literary spirit of the new fiction than Nock; from them came warnings that an indiscriminate acceptance of its picture of a thwarted America could subvert as well as further "the search for reality within the American people."

One important danger recognized was the loss of perspective on Europe. Ernest Boyd, for example, using Willa Cather's *Youth and the Bright Medusa* as a case in point, charged that American writing at the moment tended to be more pious than true on the subject of Main Street and European values:

More and more articulate becomes a generation of writers who declare that Americanism, as popularly understood, is absolutely incompatible with the development of the artist. . . . In Miss Cather's new book this conflict is the theme, and it might just as well have been entitled "America and the Bright Medusa," were it not for the exigencies of a work of fiction, which could not be handicapped with a title suitable for a volume of essays. . . . In these stories of Miss Cather's, and elsewhere in fiction and essay, the desolating blight of small-town life and the crass ignorance of the business bourgeoisie, are depicted. But what of Flaubert's Homais, of Bouvard and Pecuchet? Are they not also one hundred percenters? . . . There is a danger in overlooking the conditions against which literary America is in reaction. The bright Medusa is no less an object of suspicion amongst the mass of Europeans than in those communities which Miss Cather has so well described.[14]

Lucian Cary pointed out the possibilities for sentimentality in the small-town theme in his review of Floyd Dell's *Moon Calf*. He advanced the characterization of Felix Fay, who had

14. Ernest A. Boyd, "The New Fiction," *The Freeman*, II (Dec. 1, 1920), 286.

evaded the stereotype by being energetic enough to overcome his environment, as an object lesson in realism to the young writer of the day who says, "Give me a sensitive soul for hero and . . . I . . . will make a holiday for you. I will strip the middle west naked for you." [15]

After Mary Colum became its chief reviewer of fiction in 1921, the *Freeman* turned to an even fuller examination of the truth of the new realism and its value to American literature. "In this country the novelist who is an artist is really in a worse position than any other artist, for both the reviewers and the magazines conspire to deprive him of appreciation," she wrote, concerning the praise of such exploiters of the Middle West as Evelyn Scott and C. K. Smith, whose books she considered merely arid and clever.[16] She ridiculed Robert Morss Lovett's comparison, in the *New Republic*, of the "doom" of Alice Adams to that of Tess of the D'Urbervilles and praised the *Dial* for its discrimination in publishing Sherwood Anderson as the genuine artist among the group.[17] Her review of Anderson's *The Triumph of the Egg* in November, 1921, was quoted in part by the *Dial* editors in making their award to Anderson on the basis of his contribution to "the national consciousness." Mary Colum found in Anderson those qualities which appealed most to the artistic and psychological needs of the early twenties—his mysticism, his sense of the loneliness of American lives and his ability to express this symbolically, his very struggle toward craftsmanship which seemed in itself a virtue—and her critical estimate of him was representative of the sanction given him by the advanced writers of the decade.[18] She wrote:

15. Lucian Cary, "The Problem of the Sensitive Soul," *The Freeman*, II (Jan. 5, 1921), 403.

16. Mary Colum, "Mr. Tarkington and the Critics," *The Freeman*, IV (Sept. 28, 1921), 67.

17. *Ibid.*, p. 67.

18. Cf. Lionel Trilling's essay on Sherwood Anderson in *The Liberal Imagination*. Among Anderson's contemporaries, Robert Morss Lovett

Perhaps the first expression in fiction of that America which is a different thing from the America that was an English colonial projection is to be found in the novels of Mr. Theodore Dreiser. This book of Mr. Sherwood Anderson's, which is the expression of a people as remote from anything English as could well be imagined, makes Mr. Dreiser seem curiously old-fashioned. In books like "The Titan" and "The Financier," we had the expression of an almost purely dynamic energy, and of enormous, unsubtle vulgarities and of that quality which Catholic theologians call "invincible ignorance"; whereas we have in Mr. Anderson's new volume, "The Triumph of the Egg," a most subtle expression of emotional and spiritual energy where almost nothing happens to the characters except what happens in their minds, where external occurrences are the merest incidentals, where every story is the history of the adventures of a soul. One gets from the book the feeling of an immense struggle, as if both the author and the characters he creates had striven to shore and to consciousness out of a heavy, viscous sea. All art expression is, perhaps, just the struggle of a people in their fight for consciousness: the achievement of Mr. Anderson is that he has won for himself and the American people, out of whose life he writes, a stage of consciousness to which they had not before arrived. The men and women in his stories must be the loneliest people in literature, with little spiritual heritage; to whose forebears living meant perpetual mechanical contact with persons and things; and to whom, when they

said, for example, that his work was "animated by a singular unity of intention." It was "all a persistent effort to come to close grips with life, to master it, to force it to give up its secret." See *The Dial*, LXXII (Jan., 1922), 79. Paul Rosenfeld in the same issue (pp. 29–30) wrote of Anderson's success in using common words which symbolize objects lying "within the range of vision of those" who know offices and workshops and flats or dusty roads, barns, and farmhouses. These were the words that Dreiser tried to use and failed; Anderson made them poetry. His "writing pleases the eye. It pleases the nostrils. It is moist and adhesive to the touch, like milk." Alyse Gregory, reviewing Anderson's career for the *Dial* in 1923, speaks of his failings: his "nervous and mystical" treatment of sex, his "rhetorical self-indulgence," and "lack of aesthetic arrangement." His hold over his readers she attributes to "a certain perturbed integrity," a "thwarted, infantile idealism which seeks to construct a new salvation for the human race and cries out for new definitions, new sex emancipation." See Gregory, "Sherwood Anderson," *The Dial*, LXXV (Sept., 1923), pp. 245–46.

are thrown back on their own resources, life becomes a puzzled terror.

Although each story is widely different from another, there is all through the book a delicate thread of connexion, perhaps unconscious in the mind of the author. In each story is the same unity of emotion, the cry of characters against the winglessness of their lives—lives to which no literature has given a pattern for living, while no art has fed their emotions. It is as if all these characters, so widely different, cried in unison, "No one has given us wings for the spirit." [19]

Taken as a whole, the *Freeman's* reviewing of the new realism was representative of all the enthusiasms and qualifications of the advanced criticism of the day—from its espousal, then questioning of the modern temper represented by these novelists to the exaltation of Anderson as the genuine artist among the group.

Parallel to the interest aroused in the *Freeman* by the sociology of Main Street was an interest in publications evoking a reconsideration of America's late nineteenth-century heritage; these often served also as an opportunity for finding the "truth" at the expense of American materialism. Among such were the letters of Henry and William James and Santayana's *Character and Opinion in the United States*. The correspondence of Henry James, for example, furnished a test case for the issue of expatriation. "The national fact" remained for him "a blank wall as it were against which the powerful current of his genius broke into spray," Brooks wrote in his review, and proceeded to state the problem which he later developed in *The Pilgrimage:* "For [James], with his ineluctably complicated demands, expatriation was simply the condition of survival . . . [but] the evasion of America meant also the evasion of all the major experiences of life." [20]

19. Mary Colum, "Literature and Journalism," *The Freeman*, IV (Nov. 30, 1921), 281–82.

20. Van Wyck Brooks, "Our Illustrious Expatriate," *The Freeman*, I (April 28, 1920), 164–65. The *Freeman* printed two articles on Henry

The "case" of William James was, of course, different. It was his immersion in American life, his affirmation not his denial of it, which made him seem another victim of America's lack of maturity and wholeness, of the pressures of a business civilization. Santayana's really splendid chapter on his colleague (rather than John Macy's review of the letters) brought William James and the temper of his era into sharpest focus in the *Freeman*. Harold Stearns, in his long essay on *Character and Opinion*, picked out this portrait as the key to Santayana's characterization of America—"Protestant, romantic, rather capricious, and somewhat barbarous." [21] And, quoting from Santayana's description of the Harvard of William James and Josiah Royce, Stearns found one of the favorite dichotomies, that of truth and expediency, by which the "young intellectuals" liked to "explain" America:

As the university was a local Puritan college opening its windows to the scientific world, so at least the two most gifted of its philosophers were men of intense feeling, religious and romantic, but attentive to the facts of nature and the currents of worldly opinion; and each of them felt himself bound by two different responsibilities, that of describing things as they are, and that of finding them propitious to certain preconceived human desires.

As to the critique of the whole American milieu in *Character and Opinion*, Stearns voiced the full-throated disillusionment which often informed the combined social consciousness and agonized individualism of the "young intellectuals." He noted that Santayana, for all his perceptions about America's tendency to corrupt the spirit within her (to turn "self-trust"

James's *Letters*. In the second, by Ernest Boyd, James was used as a means of hitting out at the genteel tradition. He was a dilettante, who, having fled America, showed no "evidence of an intelligent participation in the literary and artistic life of the period." See "Henry James Self-Revealed," *The Freeman*, I (Aug. 25, 1920), 563–64.

21. All quotations from this review are taken from Harold Stearns, "Distance Lends Enchantment," *The Freeman*, II (Dec. 29, 1920), 378–81.

to "self-sufficiency," to transform "optimism, kindness and good will" into "the habit of doting on everything"), had been able to write sympathetically—because he was describing American culture before 1912, not that of 1920. He had known America in her "youth" and her "promise," but the war had "brought out our worst qualities and fixed them indefinitely." To think that in 1912 freedom of speech was "something of a reality," that there was "no such unholy alliance between commerce and the university," that it was possible to believe in progress and international peace, that personal liberty was assured, that tolerance was dominant—was to call up a dream of the past.

The publication of *The Education of Henry Adams* two years before the establishment of the *Freeman* deprived the magazine of a full-scale analysis of that magnificent criticism of American culture, but other books brought Henry Adams and his family into ken. *The Degradation of the Democratic Dogma* (1920) caused Van Wyck Brooks to make the main point of his review his opinion that "the atmosphere of the Adamses is one of profound distrust of human nature: sink yourself in it and you almost forget that life renews itself, that life is perpetually reborn in hope, good will, intelligence, love." [22] When *A Cycle of Adams Letters* appeared in 1921, the *Freeman* gave it to Constance Rourke for review, featuring it as the most important book of the week. Her essay, "The Adams Mind," was, in contrast to Brooks's characterization of the family, a modulated, penetrating, and sympathetic assessment of their intellectual position—aristocratic and rationalistic—and of their relationship to the main "experimental" line of American thought:

All the Adamses lived and worked in an atmosphere which was to them alien; the family habit of reserve and withdrawal was the replica and probably in some measure the result of an explicit sep-

22. "A Reviewer's Notebook," *The Freeman*, I (April 7, 1920), 95.

aration from American society, the society of the nineteenth century. Roughly speaking, it indicated the placing of an artistic temper in the midst of aggressive equalitarians. More exactly, it involved the conflict between a sequence of minds which passionately believed in order as a basis for thought and action, and one—the national—which believed in experiment, or at worst in *laissez-faire*. The struggle was sometimes prodigious, even tragic; it is a measure of their stature that the Adamses invariably encountered main issues. They all suffered defeat at crucial points; they considered themselves defeated. Henry Adams would doubtless have said that in his own case there was no conflict; he simply remained outside —the logical consummation of the type.

How visionary the Adamses often were, and how remote in mind from the civilization in which they lived is suggested at innumerable points in all their personal writings; but there is a certain saliency in the picture of John Quincy Adams on his way to the dedication of the Cincinnati observatory which Mr. Brooks Adams draws in his preface to "The Degradation of the Democratic Dogma." Old and tired and bewildered, pursuing a crude triumphal route, met at every point by the huzzas of the Western populace, which seemed chiefly to understand that he was an ex-President, he made the arduous journey with the abstract hope of helping to establish "science as a principle of political action." Even then such a notion was extinct, if ever it had truly existed; the rationalistic approach may always have been out of key in this country. But certainly it was a splendid and challenging dream. It is not too easy for a buoyant pragmatism to dismiss the body of thought which the Adamses have constructed—nor to meet their negations.[23]

Thus, in one of the best reviews in the magazine, the themes of alienation and commitment were brilliantly related to the American tradition. Such careful discriminations and delicate irony as Constance Rourke's must have impressed readers of the *Freeman*, where nearly every page called up in some way or another a revaluation of our culture and where there was a constant play of opposites in regard to attitudes toward society. The dogmatic disillusionment of Stearns on one page might

23. Constance Rourke, "The Adams Mind," *The Freeman*, III (March 23, 1921), 43–44.

alternate with a hopeful sociological spirit on another, and there was a third kind of temper, compounded of both, which the period made much of as "skepticism"—the belief that, bad as American civilization was, progress could be achieved by a free play of mind over her established institutions. This "skepticism" was related to "the buoyant pragmatism" of which Miss Rourke had written, but might well have turned for its "past" to the old ex-President in Cincinnati, whose address to the Astronomical Society was delivered "with the abstract hope of helping to establish 'science as a principle of political action.' "

A variety of books reviewed in the *Freeman* elicited the social attitudes of hope and skepticism which I have mentioned. Publications in the sciences, especially in psychology and anthropology, were likely to inspire a cheerful tone, as did the literature from Soviet Russia. Gregory Stragnall's review of Freud's *Introduction to Psychoanalysis*, for example, found promising connections between scientific development and social reform; not only did Freud give sound foundations for the revaluation of literature, anthropology, and drama, but his study of neurosis would enable us to make intelligent adjustments in our social structure.[24] Gorki's Preface to *World Literature*, the first catalogue of books published by the People's Commissary of Public Instruction to acquaint the Russian people with the books of the Western world, was described with the same feeling that revolutionary things had been accomplished, that his socialist's commitment to the humanizing power of literature seemed, as did Freud's method, a genuine advance along the road to cultural freedom.[25]

One manifestation of the *Freeman's* "skepticism" was the

24. Gregory Stragnall, "A Panorama of Psychoanalysis," *The Freeman*, I (Aug. 25, 1920), 572–73.

25. "A Vindication of Literature," *The Freeman*, I (July 21, 1920), 437–39.

tone that characterized the reviewing of that large number of books which the magazine thought it important to feature because they called into question, in one way or another, the institutions and ethos of capitalism.[26] In such cases the kind of writing often found in the political sections usually prevailed: in both, a liberal's awareness of social injustice was expressed by ridicule, an elaborate (and sometimes crude) irony, and a conscious judiciousness which implied rebuke to any party-line oversimplification of motives.

Robert Morss Lovett's analysis of Carnegie's *Autobiography* is characteristic. Depending for his effects upon the stereotype of the self-made man, Henry Adams's "Rule of Phase," and the pretensions of the Gilded Age, Lovett made Carnegie into a symbol of the capitalist world whose ideals, powers, and ethical limitations had produced the war. The "phases" of Carnegie's life were examined from that of "industrious apprentice" through "the golden egg period" to the period of "distribution," where Carnegie's self-made energy began to dissipate.[27] If these illustrated Henry Adams's theory of "social thermodynamics" rather than "triumphant democracy" (Lovett's only reference to Carnegie's social Darwinism), Lovett censured Carnegie mildly for his paternalistic labor politicies, spent more space satirizing his social and literary affiliations (with the Kaiser and Richard Watson Gilder), and pitied him for being the dupe of Woodrow Wilson's prom-

26. These books included, for example, the vast body of "now-it-can-be-told" literature concerning the war and the serious historical writing on this subject (which Charles Beard reviewed with so much wit and learning while he was a steady contributor to the *Freeman* in 1921), Upton Sinclair's "revelation" of the financial pressures behind the American press, books of value to the social historian (like Andrew Carnegie's *Autobiography*), and the story of a lesser self-made man, *The Americanization of Edward Bok.*

27. All quotations from this review are taken from Robert Morss Lovett, "The Industrious Apprentice," *The Freeman*, II (Jan. 19, 1921), 451–52.

ising idealism. Viewed in this familiar exposé light of the twenties, Carnegie might be said to be reduced to the stature of Edward Bok, whose business acumen and sentimentality were treated as the essence of commercialism in another review in the *Freeman*.[28]

The whole secular intellectual position of the magazine during its first two years, its bias against a business civilization, its ideal of astringent skepticism, its faith in the social sciences, found a full and provocative expression in James Harvey Robinson's *The Mind in the Making: The Relation of Intelligence to Social Reform* (1922).[29] This book was acclaimed by J. Salwyn Shapiro in the *Freeman* as a brilliant analysis of the nature and power of a radical's skeptical position—which combined a dedication to freedom with the obligation to make others see the nature of established institutions.[30] Shapiro's review placed the magazine in line with the liberal weeklies and the *Dial*, which emphasized either Robinson's iconoclastic power or his comfort to the contemporary humanist. To Hendrik Wilhelm Van Loon in the *Dial* Robinson was a man of wrath (an Achilles), his book, a "TNT of logical reasoning" which searched the present social system and left "that mushroomy excrescence as naked and exposed as a dried leaf in

28. Bok was described as a man who had never once known himself, who had never ministered to one fundamental need of humanity. His sentimentality was pointed up by a reference to the crowning desire of his career, to make Theodore Roosevelt the acting head of the American Boy Scouts. See Ernest Boyd, "Telling the Old, Old Story," *The Freeman*, II (Nov. 22, 1920), 355.

29. Morton G. White, whose *Social Thought in America* explores the relationships among Beard, Veblen, Holmes, and Robinson in formulating a style of liberal thought which "dominated America for almost half a century," speaks of the "sunny clarity" with which *The Mind in the Making* expressed certain concepts of Veblen and Dewey. See *Social Thought in America*, pp. 3, 184.

30. J. Salwyn Shapiro, "A New View of History," *The Freeman*, IV (Feb. 15, 1922), 546–48.

a botanist's herbarium." [31] To Carl Becker in the *New Republic* and to Irwin Edman in the *Nation* the author of *The Mind in the Making* was a man of reason who showed that the mind, once aware of its errors through the new science of psychology, could free itself to operate intelligently on society.[32] Shapiro acclaimed Robinson's recognition that the intellectual class—not Caesar but Marcus Aurelius—was the important factor in the making of history, and he placed Robinson among those who, like Bertrand Russell and Lowes Dickinson, had faith in human progress. It was for a conservative writer in the *American Historical Review* to comment on Robinson's limitations as a historian and to attack his politics: H. N. Gardiner's comment decried the book for its "crudities and exaggerations," for its failure to understand metaphysics and to credit the shaping disciplines of the medieval mind upon modern culture, and for its strongly radical bias.[33] The *Freeman's* full endorsement of *The Mind in the Making* marked, on the other hand, the paper's affinity with the pragmatic tradition in philosophy and with the strength and limitations of middle-class radical opinion which, operating between the poles of wrath and reason, had set out to expose the truth about our business civilization.

In the spring of 1922 some of the fiddles in the *Freeman* began to play a different tune as changes in literary interests coincided with the year which produced *The Waste Land*, *Ulysses*, the Proust vogue, *Secession*, and the *Dial* award to

31. Hendrick Willem Van Loon, "Achilles," *The Dial*, LXXII (Feb., 1922), 201–2.

32. Carl Becker, "History as the Intellectual Adventure of Mankind," *The New Republic*, XXX (April 5, 1922), 174–76; and Irwin Edman, "Making the Mind Fit the Times," *The Nation*, CXVI (Jan. 18, 1922), 75.

33. H. N. Gardiner, "The Mind in the Making," *American Historical Review*, XXVII (July, 1922), 767–69.

T. S. Eliot, which praised his excellence at the expense of a criticism concerned with "social laws, economic fundamentals, and the science of psychoanalysis." [34] In June, the *Freeman* printed a long and forceful essay by Joel E. Spingarn, called "A New Manifesto." This piece was in essence a counter-revolutionary attack on "the young intellectuals" as the spokesmen of modernity and the prophets of materialism, which Spingarn identified with "positivism, pragmatism, or neo-realism." [35] Speaking as one "who once called upon young men for rebellion and doubt," when it was necessary "to destroy the academic dry rot which was undermining the creative spirit of the nation," Spingarn now called upon them for an idealism which would make men seek truth inside the spirit of man in contrast to those who seek it outside. "Young critics," he admonished, who have become accustomed to "discussing art and philosophy in terms of that crude economic, political and psychological jargon of old-fashioned materialism" must realize that "on the ideal planes of art and thought" science has no place. Spingarn's attack on the liberal sociological spirit so recently dominant in the *Freeman's* literary criticism was the stimulus for an immediate reassertion of aesthetic values by the *Dial* and was symptomatic of a shift of wind in literary circles generally. (This is not to say that Spingarn's Crocean idealism became the dominant note; rather, it was his repudiation of a

34. The status of the social critics was, indeed, generally challenged. The publication of *Civilization in the United States* early in 1922 had signaled both the climax and the end of the prestige of the "young intellectuals." Brooks's temporary retirement from the *Freeman* in May and Nock's assumption of the literary editorship made for a change in tone even though Nock kept Brooks's staff of reviewers. In one of the "Reviewer's Notebooks" which he wrote during Brooks's absence Nock brushed off *Civilization in the United States* as inconsequential to social history. (Although Nock had always been admonitory and patronizing toward "the young," he had furthered the careers of some of them.)

35. All quotations from this essay are taken from Joel E. Spingarn, "The Younger Generation," *The Freeman*, V (June 7, 1922), 296–98.

prevailing point of view and his demand for a change that expressed the feelings of the hour.) In creative writing the force of native realism had abated somewhat; as Malcolm Cowley has pointed out, it was the works of "foreign importation" that were exciting the chief interest in America in 1922. *The Waste Land,* if it may be classified as foreign, *Ulysses,* Proust—all aroused challenging questions about tradition and experiment, and the weight of criticism gravitated, in the *Freeman* as elsewhere, to Europe.

The *Freeman's* interest in the intellectual life of France shifted from figures associated with the war generation—Anatole France, Guillaume Apollinaire, Romain Rolland, Henri Barbusse, Georges Duhamel—to a variety of poets and novelists who were considered primarily as artists, not as men of good will. There were reviews of the work of Francis Jammes, Colette, the Countess of Noailles, Charles Vildrac, Jean Paul Toulet, Marcel Schwob, Jean Cocteau, and Proust. On the whole the *Freeman's* presentation of contemporary French literature was that of a reserved middle-brow.[36] In the case of Proust a failure in understanding, a prejudice against the tone of certain great contemporary writers was pronounced.

Cuthbert Wright, reviewing *Le Côté de Guermantes* (II) and *Sodome et Gomorrhe* (I) from Paris, ridiculed Proust's pretensions and denigrated his psychology, for "to transfix" the subject of the homosexual "like some strange and ugly specimen, wriggling hideously under the pin-pricks and chloroform of a pedantic collector, is not good psychology, and, above all, is not good art." [37] To write an

36. See Bibliography for reviews of the works of these French authors written by Leon Bazalgette, Montgomery Belgim, Kenneth Burke, John Gould Fletcher, H. B. Fuller, Lewis Galantière, Lewis Gannett, Alyse Gregory, Pierre de Lanux, Dorothy Martin, Vincent O'Sullivan, Pitts Sanborn, Henry Logan Stuart, Gregory Zilboorg.

37. All quotations from this review are taken from Cuthbert Wright, "The Method of Marcel Proust," *The Freeman,* V (March 22, 1922), 45.

intensified version of the "Lonely One," contending with monsters and struggling with hostile races, and a bovine world [is surely] a legitimate subject for fiction. But to write it would require something more than a facile, and, in the long run, an exasperating literary eccentricity. It would require the mind of an artist.

Toward Proust, then, and toward the other great modern "foreign importations of moment," the *Freeman* was either hostile or skeptical. And nowhere in the magazine is a hostility toward the new, when the new is associated with experiment or with form, more strongly expressed than in Louis Untermeyer's review of *The Waste Land*. This review (interpreted as a piece of conscious and sensational enmity by a number of other critics) damned the poem as being both meretricious and wrong-headed. Untermeyer began by censuring Eliot's "cheap tricks" and accusing his admirers of "log-rolling." They had promoted the poem with "some of the most enthusiastically naïve superlatives that had ever issued from publically sophisticated iconoclasts." [38] In *The Waste Land*, Untermeyer said, Eliot had tried unsuccessfully to fuse two idioms—"the nuances of a speech that wavered dextrously between poetic color and casual conversation" on the one hand and "a harder, more cackling tone of voice . . . [a delight] in virtuosity for its own sake" on the other. The result was "a pompous parade of erudition, a lengthy extension of earlier disillusion, a kaleidoscopic movement in which the bright coloured pieces fail to atone for the absence of an integrated design." In conclusion, Untermeyer wrote:

38. All quotations from this review are taken from Louis Untermeyer, "Disillusion As Dogma," *The Freeman*, V (Jan. 17, 1923), 453. Untermeyer's review appeared soon after the *Dial* award to T. S. Eliot and makes the only direct reference (an incidental one) to it in the magazine. Brooks's editorial on *Secession* had come out the week before, and in the same issue with Untermeyer's review was an editorial by Brooks which restated his belief that a "high literature" could be produced only when writers identified themselves with the needs of society. See "Amor Fati," *The Freeman*, VI (Jan. 17, 1923), 438–39.

As an analyst of desiccated sensations, as a recorder of the nostalgia of this age, Mr. Eliot has created something whose value is at least documentary. Yet granting even its occasional felicities, "The Waste Land" is a misleading document. The world distrusts the illusions which the last few years have destroyed. One grants this latter-day truism. But it is groping among new ones: the power of the unconscious, an astringent scepticism, a mystical renaissance— these are some of the current illusions to which the Western world is turning for assurance of their, and its, reality. Man may be desperately insecure, but he has not yet lost the greatest of his emotional needs, the need to believe in something—even in his disbelief. For an ideal-demanding race, there is always one more God—and Mr. Eliot is not his prophet.

If *The Waste Land* was the most controversial work of the day, *Ulysses* was the most challenging. Published in Paris early in 1922, the book was reviewed a few months later by all the American advanced magazines. Reviewers treated it with the care and sense of discovery elicited by a difficult but undoubted masterpiece. Mary Colum tells us in her autobiography that three reviews of "bright young critics" in the United States pleased Joyce most: Gilbert Seldes's in the *Nation*, Edmund Wilson's in the *New Republic*, and hers in the *Freeman*.[39]

39. Mary Colum writes in her autobiography that her review, in the absence of Brooks, was handed in to Nock. "He bogged at printing the opening lines, a harmless enough sentence to the effect that in the next couple of decades from that time (1922) many books would be published on Joyce and *Ulysses*. He wrote me an annoyed letter saying that he was deleting these lines as they would be an exaggeration if applied to Cervantes or Tolstoy on the publication of any of their work. But later he was fond of publically quoting a version of my opening sentence and of saying how right I had been." See *Life and the Dream*, p. 306. The review as printed in the *Freeman* began: "Mr. James Joyce's 'Ulysses' belongs to that class of literature which has always aroused more interest than any other. Although 'Ulysses' is new and original in form, it is old in its class or type: it actually, if not obviously, belongs to the Confession class of literature, and although everything takes place in less than twenty-four hours, it really contains the life of a man." See *The Freeman*, V (July 19, 1922), 450. The magazine had a sort of lien on Joyce, for B. W. Huebsch was the first to publish *The*

Of the three hers was, with the exception of her appreciation of
the Irish background of the book, the least close to the artistic
sensibility of Joyce and his time. The review was a curious
combination of insight, blindness, and prejudice, and for the
task that *Ulysses* set the reviewer, a failure.

Ezra Pound, in a Paris letter to the readers of the *Dial,* had
written a preview of the book before it was generally reviewed
in America. With boldness and joy he had sketched in the issues
which were to occupy later critics—the tradition of *Ulysses,*
the literal and symbolic meaning of the characters and their
odyssey, their significance for the period, the very right of the
book to exist as literature. Pound told his compatriots that
Joyce had written the great epoch-making work on the state
of the human mind in our era. He had added "definitely to the
international store of literary technique." [40] The book, Pound
said, is an extension of Flaubert's truth about bourgeois society;
its hero, Bloom, is "*l'homme moyen sensuel* . . . Shakespeare,
Ulysses, the Wandering Jew . . . the man who believes what
he sees in the papers, Everyman and 'the goat'. . . . His
spouse," Molly, is both "Gea-Tellus" and a "coarse-grained
bitch." The form of *Ulysses* is justified by the result; if less
sure than James or Proust, this piece of fiction is "outside their
compass and orbit"—it is an "inferno" of the modern mind.
As a language experiment the novel has more meaning for
contemporary society than science, said Pound, reinforcing his
eulogy with two powerful statements defending art as knowledge: "a great literary masterwork is made for minds quite as
serious as those engaged in the study of medicine. . . . A
Fabian milk report is of less use to a legislator than the knowl-

---

*Portrait of the Artist as a Young Man.* Huebsch declined to publish
*Ulysses* without changes, however, after the *Little Review* had been
seized and confiscated by the United States authorities for printing in
1918 parts of the book which the authorities considered obscene.

40. All quotations from Pound's review are taken from Ezra Pound,
"Paris Letter," *The Dial,* LXXII (June, 1922), 623–29.

edge contained in L'Education Sentimentale and in Bovary."

This strong endorsement of *Ulysses* was a few months later complemented by Edmund Wilson in the *New Republic* and Gilbert Seldes in the *Nation*. Like Pound, Wilson and Seldes found their way into the book through Flaubert and Henry James, considering Joyce's work the culmination of a great tradition in fiction. Both reviewers, like Pound, thought that the book contained the essence of the intellectual life of their time, although for the younger men it was a more affirmative novel than Pound considered it. Seldes interpreted Joyce's picture of the average day as a symbol of the spiritual defeat of his generation, but he rejoiced that an "enormous relish and savoring of palpable actuality" made for a "tragic gaiety" that saved the book from pessimism.[41] Edmund Wilson stressed, as the central theme of the book, the father and son relationship: Stephen, the isolated artist, and Bloom, who was intelligent "in a more rudimentary form," were drawn together because, "by reason of the fact that they thought and imagined," they were both outlaws of their environment.[42] They were not "mean . . . bourgeois figures," but heroic—Stephen, a Lucifer, Bloom, a reasoning man, "humiliated and ridiculous," yet "extricating himself by cunning from the spirits which seek to destroy him." Basing his whole review on this interpretation of the characters, Wilson proceeded to a thorough examination of *Ulysses* as an organic whole, discussing the difference between Joyce's and Flaubert's methods of delineating consciousness, criticizing the overabundance of artistic ingenuity (which obscured the fact that Joyce is essentially a realistic artist) and the overly ambitious design. Through the entire review runs a sense of the tough, humane qualities of *Ulysses*, which puts

41. Gilbert Seldes, "Ulysses," *The Nation*, CXV (Aug. 30, 1922), 212.
42. All quotations from this review are taken from Edmund Wilson, "Ulysses," *The New Republic*, XXXI (July 5, 1922), 164-6.

some of the aridities of later Joyce criticism to shame. The book, Wilson concluded, is a work of high genius, whose importance seems to be "not so much in its opening of new doors to knowledge . . . as in its once more setting the standard of the novel so high that it need not be ashamed to take its place by poetry or drama."

In contrast to Pound, Seldes, and Wilson, who read the "masterwork" as a triumph of fictional art and the human spirit and as an archetype of their generation, Mary Colum, in her review in the *Freeman*, "The Confessions of James Joyce," found the tradition of *Ulysses* not in fiction but in the "confession class of literature," more specifically of the "Rousseau-Strindberg" type in contrast to the "Saint Augustine-Tolstoy type." [43] If the difference between Rousseau and Joyce is "extraordinary," the

resemblances are also extraordinary—a psychoanalyst would say they had the same complexes. Like Rousseau, Joyce derives everything from his own ego; he lives in a narrow world in which he himself is not only the poles, but the equator and the parallels of latitude and longitude; like Rousseau he has a passion, not only for revealing himself, but for betraying himself; like him also, he deforms everything he touches. Joyce's method of deforming is chiefly the sexual smear; where Rousseau romanticizes, Joyce deromanticizes. In Joyce, as in Rousseau, we find at its highest a quality which in lesser men is the peculiar fault of the literature of their time; in Rousseau this was sentimentalism, in Joyce it is intellectualism.

This analogy is one of the two main points of the review. The other, taken from the premise that *Ulysses* "gives the impres-

43. All quotations from this review are taken from Mary Colum, "The Confessions of James Joyce," *The Freeman*, V (July 19, 1922), 449–52. (One is tempted to make a point of the fact that no title other than that of the book is prefixed to the other reviews cited—as if *Ulysses* were too grand a masterpiece to submit to a Lilliputian reviewer's oversimplification.)

sion of being literally derived from experience," is a detailed explication of the Irishness of the book and the difficulties that the non-Celt and non-Catholic will have in understanding it. Stephen, with his Irish sense of death, and Bloom, who is "so real that no Dubliner can fail to recognize in him a father or an uncle," are discussed as wonderfully true racial types, "in spite of the sex-obsession with which Joyce endows him in common with all his other characters." Stephen's and Bloom's progress through Dublin is described, as well as the "remarkable" way in which "the separate subconsciousnesses of [both] are revealed, with every aimless thought, every half-formed idea and every unformed phrase indicative of their separate character and personality." But Mrs. Colum does not touch on the import of their relationship, nor does she grant the total structure of *Ulysses* "paramount literary interest." From the scene in the hospital to the end—the parodies, the catechism relating to Bloom and Stephen, the revelation of the mind of Marion Bloom—*Ulysses* is not of "artistic" but only of "scientific" interest. (The study of Mrs. Bloom, for example, would "doubtlessly interest the laboratory, but to normal people it would seem an exhibition of the mind of a female gorilla who had been corrupted by contact with humans.")

What, then, has Joyce accomplished in "this monumental" book?

He has achieved what comes pretty near to being a satire on all literature. He has written down a page of his country's history. He has given the minds of a couple of men with a kind of actuality not hitherto found in literature. He has given an impression of his own life and mind such as no writer has given before; not even Rousseau.

In conclusion, Mrs. Colum took up the current charge of obscenity against *Ulysses* and the attempts of Mr. Joyce's admirers to absolve him: "Why attempt to absolve him? It is obscene, bawdy, corrupt. But it is doubtful if obscenity in literature ever corrupted anybody." There is, however, an "alarming thing" about the book, for it shows that science is making "amazing inroads" on literature. "After Ulysses," Mrs. Colum wrote,

I can not see how anybody can go on calling books written in the subconscious method, novels. It is as plain as day that a new literary form has appeared, from which the accepted form of the novel has nothing to fear; the novel is as distinct from this form as in his day Samuel Richardson's invention was from the drama.

The questions for Joycean criticism raised by these reviews of *Ulysses* in the advanced magazines of the twenties are almost as varied as the book itself. But the issue which brings the *Freeman's* treatment of modern literature into focus is the disagreement of the reviewers about the nature of *Ulysses*—for that matter, of any work of art—as truth. In this sense Mrs. Colum's review reaffirms the limits of a social and psychological criticism which stopped short of a fundamental consideration of language and form in investigating the relation of art to reality and was thus led to deny the value of experiments which took literature out of certain traditional means of dealing with human experience. In Pound's assertion that "a Fabian milk report is of less use to the legislator than the knowledge contained in . . . Bovary" lies the essence of the critical renaissance of the early twenties and before, with all its exploration of the relationships of art and society that Pound's terms imply. At the turn of the twenties the two kinds of belief about literature, as power and as a special kind of truth, stood potentially together to form a rationale which could relate them to each other and to the whole of life. In growing further and further apart, during the *Freeman's* lifetime and after, each, in denying the other, lost the force of its beginning, and American criticism was deprived of a wholeness of vision which it has taken three decades of exploration into the "aesthetic" and the "social" at least partly to restore.[44]

44. An evaluation of the criticism of Brooks by Gorham B. Munson in 1925 illustrates the limitations of the aesthetic avant-garde. Munson, condemning Brooks as a conservative for his belief "that true criticism is . . . the intellectual study of origins and relations," also deplored the type of his literary sensibility which "has no impediments in reading Charles Dickens; it can, in fact, read him with satisfaction." See Munson, "Van Wyck Brooks: His Sphere and His Encroachments," *The Dial*, LXXVIII (Jan., 1925), 36, 39.

## Chapter Seven

# The Passing of *The Freeman*

The *Freeman* never acquired more than ten thousand sub-scribers, but it was a notable *succès d'estime*. Nock claimed for his magazine the reputation of being, among those of a cultural level able to understand it, "quite generally acknowl-edged . . . the best paper published in our language."[1] The remark is possibly hyperbolic, but it conveys an essential truth about the regard in which the *Freeman* was held by its small, varied, but mainly intellectual audience. Almost unanimously they seem to have thought that, in a period where the first duty of every critic was to be a propagandist of culture, the *Freeman*, so conscious of its mission and able to deliver a dazzling array of goods, had a striking, even unique quality. Many readers admired this quality, whether or not they agreed with the po-litical or literary policies of the paper. Santayana, who was a perspicacious and sympathetic observer of the America of his day, suggested the need which the *Freeman* filled in this country and the appeal which it made to its native readers when he wrote from abroad a congratulatory letter to the editors, which they proudly printed in a May, 1921, issue:

Far as I am from sharing its political faith, I find the *Freeman* far better written than anything I saw in my day: there is a conscious-ness in it of the world at large, and of the intellectual landscape, things which I used to miss in America altogether.[2]

Extended horizons were, of course, characteristic of ad-vanced American journalism as a whole in the early twenties. Certainly, other magazines were speaking forcefully to whom-ever they could about the rejuvenated life of the intellect and

1. Albert Jay Nock, *Memoirs of a Superfluous Man*, p. 168.
2. Quoted on the back page of *The Freeman*, III (May 18, 1921), 240.

the imagination around them—especially those periodicals with which, for their positions in advanced journalism, it has often seemed to me significant to compare the *Freeman*. Yet, none in this period of criticism, which was dedicated with singular intensity to the cultivation of a free and civilized existence for the artist and the supporting intelligentsia, gave this ideal such timely, varied, and intense expression as did the *Freeman*.

In the descriptions of the magazine by those readers and contributors who looked back nostalgically upon it, the adjective almost invariably used is "brilliant." Obviously, this word defies analysis, but the fact that it was introduced with surprising consistency tempts one to think that the epithet was not just generally honorific and that, perhaps unconsciously, it had for the men and women of the period a special meaning in relation to the *Freeman*. And one comes to believe that they called the paper brilliant because it was so precisely of its time, that is, because it aspired to ideals held dear by the cultivated American—the ideal of intellectual freedom and the ideal of distinction (Brooks's "fierce glitter of the intellect")—in a very impressive way.

None of the other journals had just the *Freeman's* direct sense of itself as being "pro culture" or of its writers as "ministers of culture," to quote phrases which often appeared on the magazine's back page, devoted to advertising the paper by constant variations, sometimes humorous, more often serious, on the value and excitement of "disinterested radical criticism." " 'Closed for the Summer' is not to be seen on Culture's Portals," readers were informed, for example, at the end of a June issue; or they were reminded that

the only propaganda the *Freeman* is interested in fostering is the pro-culture movement. No initiation-fee is demanded of those who would join; it is not even necessary to read the *Freeman* to be a good member, but reading the *Freeman* makes allegiance much easier and more pleasurable. It is not a quietistic cult, for it arouses opposition among those who hold the prejudices and superstitions that mark political, economic, theological and even aesthetic orthodoxies, hence invites attack and demands defence.[3]

Nor did any of the other magazines attempt to cover so persistently and so fully the cultural life around them. The variety of departments; the subjects of the longer articles, which, in addition to politics and the arts, treated numerous institutions and movements, supporting feminism, condemning the debasement of standards in American colleges, describing the life of migrant workers, assessing new theories in the physical sciences and economics; the running comments on manners in the "talk-of-the-town" section signed "Journeyman"; the inclusion of "works of creative imagination"; the length and vitality of the "Letters to the Editors"; the whole substantial and stimulating body of political and literary criticism—all made for a volley of ideas and issues not equaled by the forces of any of the other magazines.

The make-up and conception of the *Freeman*, and most importantly its literary skill, evoked a respect for the printed word which harked back to the nineteenth century in America, when, "in this country, as in Europe," to quote Lionel Trilling, "the man of original ideas spoke directly to 'the intelligent public,' to the lawyer, the doctor, the merchant, and even . . . to the working masses." [4] It was on this assumption that the *Freeman* intentionally operated; the fact that it did so contributed to its power to impress its readers, for this was an inspiriting answer to the leveling processes in the despised world of business journalism. The very Englishness of the format and spelling, which was taken with so much good humor,[5] simply underlined the point and need not have troubled the consciences of readers who, torn between America and Europe, could find in

3. See the back page of *The Freeman*, V (April 12, 1922), 120.
4. Trilling, *The Liberal Imagination*, p. 95.
5. See Chapter I, p. 33.

the *Freeman's* pages an essentially American awareness and the flavor of the Continent as well. The style of the *Freeman's* language, an enrichment of an urbane traditional diction for criticism, must have struck many as a heartening confirmation of the dignity of the intellectual life in a world which sadly needed it.

The urbanity of the serious writing found complementary expression in the *Freeman's* wit, another element of the magazine which made it striking and timely. There was much of Nock's mannered homeliness:

It is a pretty lucky thing [he wrote in September, 1920] that in this land of freedom we have arrangements whereby we can keep one of the Presidential candidates in jail; otherwise the campaign would unavoidably get a little flavor of reality. Brother Eugene Debs issues statements from the Atlanta penitentiary that really sound like human talk and verge dangerously close to matters that people have an interest in.[6]

And there was the type of "Current Comment," represented at its best by Geroid Tanquary Robinson's sparkling contribution to the ridiculing of President Harding, a favorite pastime of journalists:

At the review of the Grand Fleet at Hampton Roads the other day, the breaking waves dashed high, and President Harding rode upon the crest of them, singing a song of sea-power. We can hardly blame the President for having felt uplifted. With submarines nosing up out of the ocean, and dirigibles hiding the sun; with seaplanes zooming past the Mayflower's mast-head, and the continual cannonading of the dreadnaughts fairly drowning the strains of the "Star-Spangled Banner," it must have been a fine business altogether, and enough to upset anybody. Maybe Mr. Harding did not mean anything at all, then, when he addressed the following immortal words to the officers of the fleet: "The United States does not want anything on earth not rightfully our own—no territories, no payment of tribute; but we want that which is righteously our own, and, by the eternal, we mean to have that." If

6. "Current Comment," *The Freeman*, II (Sept. 15, 1920), 1.

this really does mean something, then, by the eternal, we should like to know what it is that is righteously our own, and is yet so much some one else's that we have the biggest navy on earth to haul it home for us.[7]

The *Freeman's* wit was admirably suited to its satiric purposes of exposing the folly of politicians, to the vein of skepticism in its serious literature, and to the paper's own polished tone. At its best, this wit, combining the sinewy character of good popular speech with a more formal diction, was concrete and incisive; at its worst, it was heavy-handed and pompous. Laughter of some sort was an important component of the enlightened journalism of the period, denoting, in its healthy, satiric response to a bland and lying age, the presence of a lively, assertive intelligence. Compared to the extravagance of Mencken's invectives or to the chatty "Comment" of the *Dial*, the *Freeman's* humor is measured, somewhat lacking in color and suppleness, at once less timely and more time-bound. This humor was, however, much savored in its day and greatly enhanced for its audience the force of the magazine.

But to attempt to reconstruct the effect of the *Freeman* upon its generation is to remember that none of these ways in which the magazine affirmed the high status of intellectual activity or satisfied the tastes of its audience had meaning apart from the intrinsic excellence of much of the criticism or from the aptness with which the magazine captured the spirit of intellectual freedom—that compound of discovery and revolt, of insight and unconscious prejudice, of exuberant, if sometimes indiscriminate, worship of the mind which formed the "naïveté" of critical writing of the early twenties. Edwin Muir, remembering the atmosphere in which he lived and wrote at this time, has effectively conjured up its genius:

We lived, it seems to me now, in a climate of "new ideas" and looked forward to a "new life" which would be brought about by

7. "Current Comment," *The Freeman*, III (May 11, 1921), 193.

the simple exercise of freedom, a freedom such as had never been formulated before in any times, since it too was new. We were, or thought we were, without "prejudices." We accepted everything, no matter what it might be. We were interested in psychoanalysis, not as a scientific method but as a magical process which would deliver us from our inhibitions and leave us with a freedom all the dearer because it was beyond our imagining. We did not know that the climate in which we lived was already growing colder, or if we did, we took care to keep it at the level of liberal warmth. While inflation was spreading around us like a dry rot, we thought only of a potentiality which would almost without lifting a finger, painlessly realize itself and deposit us in a new existence. Our desire for that new state, which was so clearly good since it was all freedom, seemed to give us a foretaste of it. To dream and to dream "scientifically," of such things as techniques triumphantly employed, prejudices dispelled, complexes dissolved, was to us a sort of activity which could achieve its end only by a wise suspension of all effort.[8]

The *Freeman,* while its point of view, on the whole, was more sober than Muir's and its aims more consciously directed, had seized powerfully on this idea of freedom, which was for its readers the central truth for criticism in their generation. To put it another way, as Edmund Wilson's imaginary Fitzgerald spoke for such readers in "The Delegate from Great Neck," it had been absurd for the established critics, for Babbitt and More and Sherman, to "preach discipline and restraint to a race bound hand and foot." [9]

The *Freeman's* success of merit was greater in this country than abroad (where the qualities of its breadth and style need not have been so striking), but the magazine won appreciative comment from G. Lowes Dickinson, Bertrand Russell, and

8. Muir, *Autobiography,* pp. 199–200.

9. Edmund Wilson, *Discordant Encounters,* p. 41. The famous "Delegate from Greatneck," (reprinted in *The Shores of Light*), is a revision, published in 1926, of an earlier piece, an imaginary conversation between "Mr. Van Wyck Brooks and Mr. Scott Fitzgerald," which came out in the *New Republic,* XXXVIII (April 30, 1924), 249–54.

other distinguished Englishmen, while the presence of foreign correspondents and foreign contributors to the "Letters to the Editors" attest that it made contact with the Continent. But the paper's reputation beyond the ocean fell short of its founders' expectations. In the United States the *Freeman* was highly respected by the political and aesthetic world which its contributors represented and by a smattering of workers, teachers, plain citizens, and Congressmen throughout the country. As numerous instances in the preceding chapters have shown, the magazine participated vigorously in advanced journalistic activity in New York. It made its mark there and elsewhere in many other ways. It was classed as "revolutionary" by the American Defense Society. Straight single taxers, who considered its Georgism unorthodox, found their disapproval mitigated by the fact that their philosophy was in such brilliant company. Literary-minded, wealthy physiocrats found the paper exactly to their taste. If the experimentalists, like William Carlos Williams or the painter Paul Strand, quarreled with the *Freeman's* critical assumptions, or if Hart Crane felt that its intellectualism, "where everything is all jumbled up together— politics, literature, painting, birth control," was stifling to a poet, such men read the magazine, reckoned with its influence, and contributed to it when they could.[10] Not surprisingly, it made an impression on the leading colleges and universities, from which it often drew contributors. Two pleasing stories arose about the *Freeman's* cultural status at Columbia. There is the legend that Nicholas Murray Butler, whom the paper delighted to ridicule as a pretentious, worldly-minded educator, declined to subscribe but went regularly down to the Broadway newsstand for his copy. And there is the tale that one of his most brilliant undergraduates used to buy it ostentatiously there and carry it, title-side out, to signalize his status as a highbrow.

10. Weber, ed., *The Letters of Hart Crane*, p. 59.

There is no doubt that Albert Jay Nock had fulfilled his editorial promise, that he had shown, indeed, splendid talents which were especially suited to creating the qualities of provocativeness and prestige which were the *Freeman's*. These talents, deriving from both the limitations and virtues of his personality, formed a constant controlling force that held the paper together, concentrated its energies, and stretched it to its mark. To emphasize Nock's part in the *Freeman* is not to deny the fact that Francis Neilson's English background was an important factor in the original conception of the tone of the paper, nor to forget that its greatest vitality and intellectual significance came from the literary leadership of Van Wyck Brooks, but it was Nock who subtly composed the whole impressive structure. The aim, he wrote in his *Memoirs*, was "to see whether the quality and character of the paper could be successfully held up from issue to issue. Jumping three or four hurdles of the same height is no great feat, but jumping fifty-two at a stretch is another matter." [11] Although the *Freeman* began to fall short of this goal during its last year, Nock, on the whole, succeeded. His conscious Jeffersonianism gave his staff, as has been mentioned earlier, a belief in their privileges of freedom of speech, which made it possible for them to operate with vitality and flair. So also did his genuine, if aesthetically limited, interest in the life of the mind, his delight in elegance, even his intellectual snobbery. His belief in discipline, which made him such an exacting editor, obviously kept the standard of writing in the paper high.[12] The fact that

11. Albert Jay Nock, *Memoirs of a Superfluous Man*, p. 167.

12. The story Nock tells in his autobiography of his handling of one young contributor is revealing of his sense of himself and of the magazine: "In one way, our editorial policy was extremely easy-going, and in another way it was unbending as a ramrod. I can explain this best by an anecdote. One day Miss X steered in a charming young man who wanted to write for us. I took a liking to him at once, and kept him chatting for quite a while. When we came down to business, he diffi-

he was blind to many new literary figures was deplorable; it helped to cut the paper off from new talents and restricted its influence. Yet, this same blindness toughened, in a sense, the *Freeman's* fiber and gave it a temporary strength. "I can smell out ability as quickly and unerringly as a high-bred pointer can smell out a partridge," Nock said of his qualifications as an executive on the *Freeman* and in praise of the "three super-excellent editorial minds" on the day-by-day working staff, presumably Suzanne La Follette, Geroid Robinson, and Walter Fuller. Nock delighted in claiming that they were "totally inexperienced" and could therefore operate by "intelligence" and "common sense" rather than being bound by "editorial conventions." [13] While there were stresses and strains on the *Freeman* of a serious sort, Nock was able to mold a remarkably competent editorial group, whose high sense of themselves as members of an unusual intellectual venture increased the jour-

---

dently asked what our policy was, and did we have any untouchable sacred cows. I said we certainly had, we had three of them, as untouchable and sacred as the Ark of the Covenant. He looked a bit flustered and asked what they were.

" 'The first one . . . you must have a point. Second, you must make it out. The third one is that you must make it out in eighteen-carat, impeccable, idiomatic English.'

" 'But is that all?'

" 'Isn't it enough for you?'

" 'Why yes, I suppose so, but I mean is that all the editorial policy you have?'

" ' 'As far as I know, it is,' I said, rising. 'Now you run along home and write a nice piece on the irremissibility of post-baptismal sin, and if you can put it over those three jumps, you will see it in print. . . .' The young man grinned and shook hands warmly. We got splendid work out of him. As a matter of fact, at one time or another we printed quite a bit of stuff that none of us believed in, but it all conformed to our three conditions. . . . Ours was old-school editing, no doubt, but in my poor judgment it made a far better paper than more stringent methods have produced in my time." See *Memoirs of a Superfluous Man*, p. 172.

13. *Ibid.*, p. 170. Actually they were experienced.

nal's *élan.* His hunting metaphor is characteristic of his turn of mind and a just bit of self-revelation from this man who constantly beat the field of manners and, according to his lights, searched out distinction in a world which put it at a premium.[14]

The Neilsons also contributed to keeping up the morale of the *Freeman* and maintaining the high style in which it began. Francis Neilson made foreign contacts for the paper on the trips which they took abroad; when they were in New York, as it was their habit to be for several winters in order that they might look after their venture, Mrs. Neilson gave a number of quite grand dinners to which were invited visiting intellectuals from the Continent, various American editors, publishers, and writers, members of the *Freeman* staff, and some of its contributors. There was also an annual March birthday dinner for the paper, held at the Hotel LaFayette. This was an intimate affair, including only the founders, members of the staff, a few steady contributors, and one or two outsiders. The first of these dinners was the happiest, since it celebrated a successful paper and the only really harmonious year in the joint editorship of Nock and Neilson. Everybody made speeches; a parody of the magazine, a small printed replica called *The Freeman, jun.,* lay at each plate.[15] It is remembered that Van Wyck Brooks, whose natural eloquence was of the pen, rose, blushed, stammered a few words, and sat down; that Charles Nagel, an outsider and a former Secretary of Commerce in Taft's cabinet, spoke at length on the excellence of the *Freeman,* praising especially Nock's editorship. The parody of the magazine, mostly the work of Walter Fuller, listed a table of contents which included for "Topics of the Day" editorials called "Mens Sana in Corpore Sano," and "Where Can a Young

14. Cf. Van Wyck Brooks's remark: "It was his [Nock's] insistence on the question of improving our quality of life that made the *Freeman* so exciting." See Brooks, *Days of the Phoenix,* p. 60.

15. B. W. Huebsch has preserved a copy of *The Freeman, jun.*

Man Go?"; for the middle articles, "On Making Your Own," by Harold Stearns, "Ptomaine Street," by Sinclair Lewis Mumford, and "The Autocracy of Service," by Warren Gamaliel Harding. For "Letters" there was listed "A Home Brew," by H. L. Mencken; for "Poetry," "Artichokes and Amethysts," by Amy L.; for "Books," "The Follies of 1925," by Brander Matthews, and "The Gentle Art of Making Puns," by B. W. Huebsch. "Current Comment" reported the election of Albert Jay Nock to the Presidency of the United States on the ticket of the United Bolters, Neilson's appointment as his Secretary of State, Harold Stearns's acceptance of the post of Commissioner of the Port. "The Reviewer's Dope Book" referred to "Eight Democratic Years," by "W. W.," and announced that a criticism befitting the dreariness of the work would appear in a later issue. In an editorial apology, "Pro Mea Vita," the *Freeman, jun.* proclaimed: "Today this paper waits with its back to the soil for the time when everybody will have abundance and leisure to do the same." This was all great fun, but the dinner sowed the seeds of discord, Neilson says, for Charles Nagel's speech "told the gathering about all the wonderful things Albert Jay Nock had performed. This started the rumor that Nock was the *Freeman*." [16] Neilson rose at once "to inform the gentleman that all the staff, including Mr. Huebsch, were editors and that no person connected with the paper should be singled out as deserving the only laurel wreath." [17]

Neilson's relation to Nock and the *Freeman* turned out to be of the utmost significance to its material welfare and the factor of most importance in its organizational history, which was relatively simple during the four brief years of its intense intellectual life. Nearly all of these events have been referred to and their effect has been discussed. They may be summarized briefly. B. W. Huebsch, Suzanne La Follette, Geroid Robin-

16. Neilson, *The Story of "The Freeman,"* p. 30.
17. *Ibid.,* p. 31.

son, and the two secretaries, Miss McMillan and Miss Taussig, stayed with the paper throughout. Walter Fuller, who had been the paper's chief wit and chief rewrite man, decided to return to England in the spring of 1922; an excellent journalist and political analyst, Harold Kellock, a steady contributor to the paper from the start, became an editor in Fuller's place. William MacDonald, another political writer, was closely associated with the editorial work, but his name never appeared on the masthead. Brooks's leave of absence and Nock's literary editorship from May, 1922, to January, 1923, have been discussed, as well as the gradual lessening of Brooks's editorial and writing activity after his return. Suzanne La Follette, Nock's special pride and able disciple, assumed the directing editorship on two occasions, the first when Nock took over from Brooks, the second when Nock, for a period of three months in the beginning of 1923, went to Germany, in ill health and tiring of his job, leaving word "that the paper should not be sent him and that no one should write him any letters under any circumstances." [18] Neilson, who had stipulated at the first that he should not be tied down by the enterprise and who, with his wife, had designated Nock as the *chargé d'affaires*, nevertheless spent the whole of the first year of the paper in cooperation with the editorial staff and in supplying material for nearly every issue. A six months' trip abroad with Mrs. Neilson, beginning in the spring of 1921, broke this active participation. Although he sent in material from Europe, he wrote less and less frequently for the magazine, until, after the third year, his work disappeared almost altogether. It is believed that this situation was the primary factor in the *Freeman's* cessation, causing Mrs. Neilson, when she realized that the paper was no longer in any sense her husband's, to withdraw her support.

The course of Neilson's relation to the paper gouged very

18. Albert Jay Nock, *Memoirs of a Superfluous Man*, p. 173.

deeply into his psyche, as his disillusioned, resentful *Story of "The Freeman"* and even the later toned-down account of the magazine in his autobiography show. About his participation as a whole he made several statements: that he had never consented to devote his whole time to the paper, but that Nock was continually pumping him for ideas; that he (Neilson) had yielded to his wife's wishes to go abroad the second spring in which the *Freeman* was in operation because he thought that the paper was launched and could get on without him; that Nock was aghast at his departure because the supply of ideas might be cut off; that he (Neilson) did not regard himself as more than a feeder of ideas and that anyone was welcome to take the material he sent in and make the best use of it for the paper; that he constantly sent in material which was not used or was appropriated by Nock.[19] The implication in the *Story of "The Freeman"* particularly was that Nock used the *Freeman's* sponsor to promote his own success. Yet, even in the white heat of the former account, Neilson declared (without irony) that Nock was a masterful editor. Evidence from other members of the staff adds up to the opinion that Neilson, for all that he was a worthy man, was outclassed by Nock and was neither able nor inclined to write with the care that the standard of the *Freeman* demanded. The whole business is distressing (and probably more complicated and emotionally charged than we know), but two clear points emerge: that something in Nock's behavior outraged Neilson, and that he lacked the ability and drive, even the wish, to be the head of the *Freeman;* yet his pride was terribly hurt that such an important and successful enterprise should not, in the intellectual sense, belong to him.

Mrs. Neilson had, as we know, agreed to a full subsidy of the magazine for three trial years. Before they were up, her

19. See Neilson, *The Story of "The Freeman,"* pp. 27–32; *My Life in Two Worlds,* II, 41–42.

pleasure in the paper had begun to wane as the suspicions and recriminations grew. But, when the time came to make a decision about the continuation of the *Freeman*, she consented to finance it for another year. One reason was the fact that her interest was somewhat revived when, in the fall of 1922, she herself became a literary contributor to the magazine. Perhaps her work was accepted with a wry smile at commercial pressures: "October in Arcady," the first of eight stiff, conventional little sketches, appeared in the appropriate month of that year and was followed by others at two- or three-monthly intervals until the paper ceased publication.[20] The stretch from March, 1923, to March, 1924, was the *Freeman's* last year. Despite Mrs. Neilson's participation, she and her husband were seriously disaffected, while there were signs of flagging energy within the working staff and within the corpus of the magazine itself. Nock was ill and tired, Brooks was no longer a constant participant, the inclusion of a large body of serial writings in the weekly issues, although such writing was of high caliber, reduced the tempo of the originally rapid exchange of ideas and slowed the march of names across the *Freeman's* pages. The magazine had never begun to pay for itself, but Neilson says that his wife had not expected it to, indeed, would not have touched the paper if "she had thought for a moment that it was to be a commercial enterprise." [21] Relations between Nock and the Neilsons became increasingly strained in the fall of 1923. In February, 1924, a disagreement over the management

20. Neilson describes the circumstances as follows, inaccurately placing the printing of the first sketch in the winter of 1923–24: "One day Helen showed me a piece she had written and asked if I would make suggestions about improving it. It was so good that I decided to take it to the *Freeman*, and have it published. When I showed the article to Nock, he would not believe she had written it." Neilson says that the publication of the piece was a delightful surprise to Mrs. Neilson, for "she had never dreamed that she would see an article of hers in print." See *My Life in Two Worlds*, II, 68–69.

21. Neilson, *The Story of "The Freeman*," p. 48.

of the office and a belief that Nock was too ill to carry on caused Neilson to ask his wife to terminate the magazine.[22]

The announcement that the *Freeman* would discontinue publication with the March 5th issue (and its 208th number) of 1924 was commensurate in dignity to the prospectus of the new magazine which had come into being four years earlier and, indeed, to the dignity of the honorable position which it had won for itself as a journal of opinion. That the news of the *Freeman's* closing would be received with regret by most of its readers, the editors did not doubt:

In four years the *Freeman* has become a fellowship of fine minds in all parts of the globe, and we humbly believe that with its passing a vitalizing force passes.

For four years this experiment in publishing an absolutely free paper, whose views on public questions were grounded in a sound philosophy, whose principles of life and art were those of enlightened, radical men and women who regard change as a law of growth, has been conducted disinterestedly, with unusual devotion, by workers who looked for no profit other than that implicit in the work itself. . . .

The paper was a gift to the American people, a gift as real as hospitals, laboratories, colleges, and other public services supported by wealthy citizens, and more valuable from the point of view of civilization than many of these.

The *Freeman* is a success: an organ of critical opinion is possible if people want it. Having proved what can be done, the *Freeman* retires at the highest point of its circulation, confident that its eight volumes represent a valuable contribution to journalism, a proof of the potential capacity of America in culture, and a worthy token of its founder's citizenship. Helen Swift Neilson, who, for the first time since the inception of the *Freeman*, permits her name to be used, agreed to support the *Freeman* for three years, during which time it was hoped that a body of readers sufficiently large to justify a continuance would be found. She voluntarily added one year to that gift; and now as the paper ceases to be she joins with the editors and the publisher in thanking the friends whose favour and

22. *Ibid.*, p. 49.

co-operation it has found. Their compensation lies in the knowledge of what the *Freeman* has meant to thousands during four years, and a fuller reward will come when the American people, wanting a magazine of ideas, imagination and humour, will turn back to the *Freeman* for inspiration and for a pattern.[23]

This notice, unsigned, was composed by B. W. Huebsch for the issue of February 6, 1923.

The *Nation* and the *New Republic* wrote serious and courteous editorials on the announcement of the passing of the *Freeman*. Weighing all differences with their "radical" opponent as insignificant in comparison to the blow which the cessation of such a distinguished paper dealt to the "weekly field of journals of opinion," both magazines attempted to define the *Freeman's* character in relation to the current state of American culture, for they saw in the limited circulation the paper had achieved and in its demise a sad comment on the American public.[24] Although both spoke of the superiority of the literary material over the political, it was to the paper's political position that the liberal magazines gave most heed. The *Nation* hoped that the excellent capabilities of Nock as an editor would be put to use elsewere.

On the question of the *Freeman's* place and reputation in America, the *Nation* wrote that, although the emphasis on the "land panacea" was a limiting factor in its political significance, the failure of the *Freeman* was, nonetheless, a symptom of America's "political backwardness" and "lack of interest in fundamental reform," as well as of her denial of the value of self-criticism.[25] The *New Republic*, in an illuminating analysis of the *Freeman*, designated intelligence as the outstanding char-

23. "A Last Word to Our Readers," *The Freeman*, VIII (Feb. 6, 1924), 508.

24. The public in general inferred from the editorial announcement in the *Freeman* that the reason for its closing was the failure of the magazine to support itself, at least in part, by its subscriptions.

25. "The Freeman," *The Nation*, CXVIII (Feb. 6, 1924), 131.

acteristic of the paper, yet noted that there were many more intelligent Americans than there were subscribers.[26] This fact threw "light on the quality of the *Freeman* and upon the American mind." The *Freeman* was outside the main current of American thought in two important respects, the *New Republic* maintained. For one thing, the editors' theory of the state, "that the state is maintained by an exploiting group alien in social status, if not in blood, to the great mass of the people," and that the state must be abolished "by the development of ideas that will leave it high and dry," was contrary to the dominant force of progressive liberalism which would strengthen the state for "the protection of the weak against the strong" and was also contrary to the desire for political action in an essentially practical people. Second, the *New Republic* said, the *Freeman's* constant tone of disillusionment about politics was repugnant to Americans, for "a constructive superstition" had fastened itself upon the country.[27] "Disillusionment is of all kinds of like-mindedness the weakest cohesive force," the *New Republic* pointed out; therefore for the paper's welfare and for its usefulness to America it was unfortunate that the *Freeman* had "given politics the first place in the book and a generous share of its space . . . and had allowed itself to be thought of as a political journal whose position was anti-political." But, whatever its shortcomings, the magazine's concern with

the unconscious processes of adjustment of the individual to social needs and of society to individual needs; the educational process taken as a whole, the conquest of new knowledge; the evolution of the unwilling, suspicious, half servile laborer into the free co-operator

26. See "The Passing of the Freeman," *The New Republic,* XXXVIII (March 5, 1924), 33–34.

27. A writer to the *New Republic* letter column spoke thus of the cessation of the *Freeman:* "I tried hard several times to be one of the 30 per 100,000 to support the *Freeman.* But because of its self-satisfied

seemed so important to the *New Republic* that it "welcomed the presence of an organ so intent upon them that it could only see gray in politics." Thus did this journal of progressive political liberalism lay stress on the essentially cultural significance of its rival and, one notes, found the *Freeman's* worth in its affinity—despite its "radicalism"—with the whole ethos of liberal culture in the early twenties.

The *Dial*, speaking later than the *New Republic* and the *Nation* on the place of the *Freeman*, regretted that its demise had left America with only five readable magazines, "five gems" on "the five digits" of Columbia's "patriotically mottled hand": the *Dial*, "lambent on the index finger," the *Nation* and the *New Republic* "in the safe middle (as usual)," the *Yale Review* "on the thumb," which never points, and "on the little finger *Vanity Fair*." The *Freeman* had occupied the other "go-getting instrument"—perhaps intentionally not designated as either right or left.[28]

After the announcement of its impending end in mid-February, the magazine came to a close very quickly. Loyal subscribers (the *New Republic* believed that no paper had more devoted ones) rushed forward with offers of financial support, among them the rich Philadelphians, Mr. and Mrs. Edmund Cadwallader Evans and Mrs. Evans's sister, Miss Ellen Winsor, who later became the friends and patrons of Albert Jay Nock [29]

---

certainty that the world is made up of omniscient angels and natural fools, the former being limited to its editors and contributors and the latter embracing the rest of the known world, I gave it up." See William Clark Trow writing from Cincinnati to the *New Republic*, XXXVII (Feb. 20, 1924), 338.

28. "Comment," *The Dial*, LXXVI (May, 1924), 469.

29. Miss Winsor describes their interest in the paper and the meeting with Albert Jay Nock as follows: "Then came the appalling news the *Freeman* was to cease publication. We hastened to New York to help in any way we could to save it. . . . There sat Albert Jay Nock—his superb head, the head of an aristocrat and scholar, outlined against a window. His blue eyes were like steel. They pierced us through and

and who subsidized the writing of Suzanne La Follette's *Concerning Women* (1926). But the Neilsons declined all offers of aid, and there was apparently no effort to organize the paper under another name. The last number of the *Freeman* went to press on March 4—on a Tuesday, as was its custom. "It was on a Friday evening," Nock writes, "that we of the staff bade one another farewell; at eleven o'clock the next morning, when the Dutch liner *Volendam* moved out of her slip, I was aboard her on my way to Brussels." [30] The Neilsons made final arrangements with the staff and, after this time, never saw Nock again. The expert accountant from Swift and Company who had been in charge of the books took away his records; the offices at 116 West 13th Street were closed down; B. W. Huebsch, when he moved his publishing business uptown, destroyed the files of the *Freeman's* correspondence; and, to borrow a friendly phrase from the *Dial*, the "somewhat *rural* but essentially *cultivated*" *Freeman* was no more.[31]

It is not surprising that the intelligentsia in 1924 should have attributed the passing of the *Freeman* to the mental sluggishness and conformity of American readers, that the mourning should, in fact, have expressed itself in the rituals of a criticism whose main concern for a decade had been the need for and dangers to a new intellectual life in the United States. Nock, formalizing the issue of the *Freeman's* closing with his characteristic assurance, described the course of the magazine as an experiment in measuring "the general level at which the best culture in the country stood"; he offered the paper's small distribution as a proof that the test, from the point of view of "the public

---

through and found all their owner wished to know." See Garrison, ed., *Letters from Albert Jay Nock to Edmund C. Evans, Mrs. Edmund C. Evans and Ellen Winsor*, Introduction.

30. Albert Jay Nock, *Memoirs of a Superfluous Man*, p. 174.
31. "Comment," *The Dial*, LXXVI (May, 1924), 469.

mind," had been "launched . . . under as unfavorable circumstances as could well be imagined." [32] Even the *New Republic*, with its realistic analysis of the *Freeman's* uncongeniality to Americans (an analysis which held as true for the approximately thirty or forty thousand subscribers to the liberal weeklies as for the whole of America), had emphasized its regret that the public was unwilling to support, for the value of its intransigence and its cultural criticism, a journal of protest which went against the grain of practically-minded American thought. The *Freeman*, then, by the very shortness of its existence, by its eccentricity, by its meaning to its generation as a brilliant expression of our cultural aspirations, provided intellectuals with a most usable symbol of the conflict between themselves and the rest of America, a conflict in which they saw themselves as likely to be defeated.

This interpretation of the *Freeman's* history has an essential rightness, even if we know that, but for its internal situation, the magazine might have continued its way for some time to come. The fact that the paper succeeded in merit only is representative of the fate that has often befallen journals of quality in this country, in the twenties and before and after. From the perspective of thirty years, however, it is apparent that the *Freeman* had filled its place in the decade and, without a decided change of nature, could not have maintained for very much longer the position of prestige that it held. As has been suggested earlier, its readers valued the magazine because it was so eminently of its period; more accurately, if the changes within the paper's brief span of four years are carefully weighed, the *Freeman's* greatest power lay in expressing the critical rationale at the turn of the twenties, in responding, that is, to a tide of feeling which was social in orientation, which came from a belief in the possibilities of an intellectual enlightenment, which was sloughing off an unsatisfactory po-

32. Albert Jay Nock, *Memoirs of a Superfluous Man*, p. 167.

litical liberalism in search of a better, and which was committed to the arts in the way of Brooks and Bourne. It was a
transitional time and a transitional approach to American culture that the *Freeman* reflected more strongly than did any of
the other advanced magazines of the period. When the weekly's
political cynicism lost pungency, when a personal rather than
a social individualism took over among intellectuals and the
"European toot" became for a time expressive of the spirit of
the twenties, when the limitations of Brooks's leadership in
letters were shown up, when the newer, more extravagant
language of the avant-garde proclaimed that there was more
depth and range in contemporary literature than the *Freeman*
cared to look for—then this magazine began to lose its influence over the intellectual group whose consciousness of itself the paper had helped to form. The turn had actually begun before the *Freeman's* existence was half over. During the
first two years the movement was forward and affirmative;
afterward, despite the increasing wealth of the material on the
arts, which compensated in part for the lessening vitality of
the political sections, and despite the excellence and oftentimes
greater expertness of the literary criticism, the magazine played
either a static or a negative role. That it continued to be a
focus for cultural activity is, of course, true, as is the fact that
it stood out as a sort of monument to intellectual distinction.
But, for all its elegance and eclecticism, the *Freeman* had fairly
bristled with the character of the very early twenties, when
the best criticism, facing the whole of American life, was often
an emphatic expression of incomplete truths—but said for the
right reasons. The *Freeman* had, indeed, been so much of that
time and of that place which bridged the period between the
older advanced opinion of the prewar years and the reassertions of intellectual freedom after the war that one feels it
could belong to no other.

By 1924 it was possible for the *Freeman*, deprived of a

rapport with the times which was its driving force, to distribute, as it were, many of its functions among its colleagues or to will them to periodicals which were to come soon after. The *Dial* had already assumed the leadership in literary journalism. There was little in the way of invective against the stupidity of a mass civilization that H. L. Mencken, in his new magazine, *The American Mercury* (1924), could not, simply because he was a more talented writer, do better than Nock. Some of the *Freeman's* sophistication, wit, and verbal precision, its picture of city life, and its sense that there was a social comedy in America which could be represented with urbane irony appeared in a livelier form when the *New Yorker* began publication in 1926 to shock the old lady from Dubuque.

In their farewell to the public the *Freeman's* editors had expressed the hope that it would serve as an inspiration and a pattern for future magazines of "ideas, imagination, and humor." No paper during the twenties or later fully revived the scope or intention of the original; however, at the beginning of the new decade, and of the Depression, an attempt was made to recapture the spirit of the *Freeman* as a radical journal of opinion along the old lines. The *New Freeman*, edited by Suzanne La Follette, in association with Albert Jay Nock and Ernest Boyd, and sponsored by a wealthy chemist, Peter Fireman, was published for a little over a year, from March, 1930, to May, 1931. Using a modified version of the old *Freeman's* policy and organization, this later magazine printed work by some of the old contributors—Mumford, Arvin, Mason, Muir; Nock wrote the "Miscellany"; Ernest Boyd, a weekly literary column; the "Current Comment" imitated its model in dealing tartly with the political events of the moment. Although the *New Freeman* also dissociated itself from liberalism, the paper did not revive its predecessor's "sophisticated single-tax" slant, as it had come to be called. What political policy can be discerned recalls the old *Freeman's* distrust of imperialism and its defense of civil liberties and of the Soviets. In the sober light of the thirties the rights of Communists and of Russia loomed large as issues, as the paper's newer radicalism veered towards a Marxist decade. The *New Freeman*, like its predecessors radical in politics and the arts, was a creditable magazine, but, lacking in fire, richness and a real *raison d'être*, it only partly reproduced the aura of the old.

The journalistic tradition of the *Freeman* as a reflector of enlightened liberal culture ends with this magazine of the early thirties. Although the name has been given to several magazines since that time—always with a thin thread of connection—none falls, except with the greatest literalness of interpretation, within the radius of the journal that Nock and Neilson founded. The first of these magazines, an orthodox single-tax organ, the *Monthly Freeman*, published in the later thirties by the Roger Schalkenback Foundation and the Henry George School, made no impression outside strict Georgist circles.

The second set of *Freemans*, as they may for convenience be called, originated in 1950, and they have continued to the present, without a break but with three changes in organization. Each, in its own way, represents a form of social criticism, diminished and gone sour, in which, as Richard Hofstadter puts it (describing a familiar pattern in American political history), "the impulses behind yesterday's reform" are "enlisted in the service of reaction." [33] The *Freeman* which appeared in 1950 was backed by Alfred Kohlberg, a linen importer connected with the China lobby; the editorial board consisted at that time of Henry Hazlitt, John Chamberlain, and Suzanne La Follette. Miss La Follette (whose political sympathies had moved from philosophical anarchism in the twenties to Trotsky or forms of anti-Stalinism in the thirties and forties to libertarian conservatism by 1950) was responsible for the use of the name and for the format, which imitated

33. Hofstadter, *The Age of Reform*, p. 21.

certain features of the first *Freeman*. Announcing its policy as a defense of traditional (laissez-faire) liberalism, this magazine of the fifties began as a journal of protest for disaffected liberals, like Hazlitt and Chamberlain, for anti-Stalinists, like Miss La Follette, and for partisans of General MacArthur. Reflecting the reactionary hysteria of the McCarthy era, this *Freeman* split—but did not immediately discontinue—on the question of the editorial tone with which New Deal liberalism was to be discredited.[34] In July, 1954, this *Freeman* was reorganized with a new sponsor as *The Freeman: A Monthly for Libertarians.* Published by the Foundation for Economic Education, this magazine, with Frank Chodorov, a disciple of Nock, as its editor, stood for the "rights of the individual, the free market, private property, and limited government." [35] Its announced intention was "to argue for libertarianism and make a profit." ("Above all things," its publisher declared, "the *Freeman* will not present 'both sides.' Let the Socialists state their case as they see it. Their press is adequate.") It is this version of the *Freeman*, with its roster of conservative contributors, Eugene Lyons, Max Eastman, and William Buckley among them, that made the strongest bid for a new conservative press of the type now represented by the *National Review*. The *Freeman*, in its next form, the present *Freeman: A Monthly Journal of Ideas on Liberty*, took shape in January, 1956, without an editorial masthead but with Henry Hazlitt and John Chamberlain again to the fore. Primarily an outlet for conservative economic opinion and still backed by the

34. Henry Hazlitt, a more moderate antiliberal than his colleagues, was put off the board in March, 1952, only to be reinstated in January, 1953, when the directors of the magazine declined to sanction the policy of Chamberlain and Miss La Follette. These two left the magazine. See "The New Freeman," *Time*, LVI (Oct. 16, 1950), 46–49; and "Battle for the Freeman," *Time*, LXI (Jan. 26, 1963), 74–75.

35. All quotations concerning the editorial policy of the magazine are taken from Leonard Read, "From the Publisher," *The Freeman*, V (July, 1954), 5.

same publisher, the magazine is reduced both in size and in scope. Traces of the original *Freeman* reappear: there is a "Reviewer's Notebook," and Nock turns up now and then as a patron saint. The whole thing strikes a quiet note, is staid and dry.

While the name of the *Freeman* in the course of three decades of violent political disruption has come to stand for a kind of journalism which, stripped of the openness, balance and humane convictions of the original, has developed (or rather restated) the least viable elements of the original magazine, the memory of the *Freeman* of the early twenties remains a small but warm one. "I still see it mentioned once in a while . . . with some little touch of affection," [36] Nock wrote in 1943, two years before his death. His comment, taken in connection with the description earlier in this chapter of the *Freeman's* effect upon its contemporaries, suggests what still seems to be true, that a knowledge of the paper survives largely in the nostalgia of the individuals who wrote for it or read it at the time of its publication. That a magazine which is intrinsically so good and so representative of a turning point in American cultural history should have won such minor notice from literary and cultural historians is puzzling. The major book which attempts to treat comprehensively the history of American periodicals up to the present day does not mention the *Freeman*.[37] Elsewhere, receiving slight attention, it has often been the victim of a gremlin-like misrepresentation; for example, Allan Nevins's *American Press Opinion* said it wanted to be called "liberal"; the *Literary History of the United States* named Randolph Bourne as one of the founders. Among

36. Albert Jay Nock, *Memoirs of a Superfluous Man*, p. 168.
37. I refer to Wood, *Magazines in the United States*. However, there is a short, accurate representation of the *Freeman* in Theodore Bernard Peterson, *Magazines in the Twentieth Century* (Urbana, Ill., University of Illinois Press, 1956).

the intellectual histories of America which have appeared over the years, none has dealt specifically with the *Freeman's* point of view, and only Daniel Aaron's *Writers on the Left* (1961) has turned to the *Freeman* for a substantial body of source material to illuminate an interpretation of social thought in the 1920s. Thus, the *Freeman* has not found a place in the canon of the liberal tradition, nor has it been recognized by those liberal critics who question the tradition from within. On the contrary, the magazine has been perpetuated by journals close in spirit to the *National Review* and honored in Russell Kirk's evocation of the religious conservative mind. To say that it truly does not belong in this company is not to overlook the essentially retrospective and cranky quality of the original magazine's professed radicalism or its scorn of a mass culture or its hostility to progressive liberalism. Rather, it is to emphasize the fact that the *Freeman* derived its greatest strength from another source. The secular, naturalistic, reform spirit of the early twenties shines through its liveliest, best pages and illuminates its best writers.

# Appendix

Prospectus of *The Freeman*, "a new national weekly," which appeared as a full-page advertisement in the *New Republic* on February 18, 1920.

In March, Mr. B. W. Huebsch will begin to publish *The Freeman*, a new weekly edited by Mr. Francis Neilson and Mr. Albert Jay Nock. *The Freeman* is planned to meet the new sense of responsibility and the new spirit of inquiry which recent events have liberated, especially in the fields of economics and politics. It will follow developments in all phases of international life and its point of view, in the discussion of industry and commerce, will be that of fundamental economics. In dealing with public affairs it will concern itself more with the principles of politics than with political events, personalities or superficial issues; and especially with the economic principles that underlie politics.

*The Freeman* will be more interested in discovering popular sentiment than in creating it and will aim rather at enlightening and unifying public opinion than at controlling or instructing it. It is grounded in the belief that the greatest public service that can be performed at this time is the promotion of free popular discussion, and that a paper which desires disinterestedly to serve its age can do no better than to take this for its avowed function.

In its treatment of news *The Freeman* will not in any sense compete with the daily newspaper or with any weekly résumé of news. Nor will it pretend to compete with such organs of special opinion as are now serving a large public and serving it exceedingly well.

*The Freeman* will also present sound criticism, freely expressed, upon literature and the fine arts, besides offering American and foreign works of creative imagination. The editors expect to make a paper which shall so far differ from existing periodicals in style and temper as well as in content and purpose as to keep out of their field; and they are confident that the venture will in time attract a public of its own which shall be sufficient to warrant its continuance.

The subscription rates were announced as $6.00 a year, $6.50 in Canada, and $7.00 in other foreign countries. A ten weeks' trial subscription was to be had for $1.00.

# Bibliography

Aaron, Daniel. Writers on the Left: Episodes in American Literary Communism. New York, Harcourt, Brace and World, 1962.

"After the Battle" [an editorial on Henri Barbusse], The Freeman, I (Jan. 23, 1920), 343-44.

Allen, Charles. "The Advance Guard," The Sewanee Review, LI (Summer, 1943), 411-29.

Allen, Frederick Lewis. Only Yesterday. New York, Harper, 1931.

—— The Big Change: America Transforms Itself, 1900-1950. New York, Harper, 1952.

"Announcement" [of the Dial award], The Dial, LXX (June, 1921), 730-32.

Austin, Mary. Earth Horizon. Boston, Houghton Mifflin, 1932.

Barker, Charles Albro. Henry George. New York, Oxford University Press, 1955.

Barker, Ernest. Political Thought in England, 1848 to 1914. 2d ed. New York, Oxford, 1950.

Barnes, Harry Elmer, and Merriam, Charles Edward, eds. A History of Political Theories: Recent Times. New York, Macmillan, 1924.

Bazalgette, Leon. "Comrades at the Crossroads" [a review of publications by Duhamel, Chennevière, Vildrac, Spiro, Romains, Durtain], The Freeman, III (July 27, 1921), 474-75.

Becker, Carl. "History as the Intellectual Adventure of Mankind," The New Republic, XXX (April 15, 1922), 174-76.

—— "What We Didn't Know Hurt Us a Lot," The Yale Review, XXXIII (March, 1944), 385-404.

Belgim, Montgomery. "A French Master of Fantasy" [Jean Paul Toulet], The Freeman, IV (Jan. 18, 1922), 453-54.

Blum, W. C. [John Sibley Watson]. "American Letter," The Dial, LXX (May, 1921), 562-68.

Bosanquet, Bernard. The Philosophical Theory of the State. London, 1899.

Bourne, Randolph. History of a Literary Radical and Other Essays. Ed. by Van Wyck Brooks. New York, Huebsch, 1920.

—— Untimely Papers. Foreword by the ed., James Oppenheim. New York, Huebsch, 1919.

"Briefer Mention" [of Main Street], *The Dial*, LXX (Jan., 1921), 106.

Brooks, Van Wyck. America's Coming-of-Age. New York, Huebsch, 1915.

—— Days of the Phoenix: The Nineteen-Twenties I Remember. New York, Dutton, 1957.

—— Letters and Leadership. New York, Huebsch, 1918.

—— The Confident Years. New York, Dutton, 1952.

—— John Addington Symonds: A Biographical Study. New York, Kennerley, 1914.

—— The Ordeal of Mark Twain. New York, Dutton, 1920.

—— The Pilgrimage of Henry James. New York, Dutton, 1925.

—— Scenes and Portraits: Memories of Childhood and Youth. New York, Dutton, 1954.

—— Sketches in Criticism. New York, Dutton, 1932.

—— Three Essays on America. New York, Dutton, 1934.

—— The World of H. G. Wells. New York, Kennerley, 1915.

Burke, Kenneth. "André Gide, Bookman," *The Freeman*, V (April 26, 1922), 155–57.

—— "The Bon Dieu of M. Jammes," *The Freeman*, III (May 11, 1921), 211–12.

Carnegie, Andrew. The Autobiography of Andrew Carnegie. Boston, Houghton Mifflin, 1930.

Chamberlain, John. Farewell to Reform: Being a History of the Rise, Life and Decay of the Progressive Mind in America. 2d ed. New York, Liveright, 1932.

Chase, Richard. The Democratic Vista: A Dialogue on Life and Letters in Contemporary America. Garden City, N.Y., Doubleday, 1958.

Colum, Mary. Life and the Dream. Garden City, N.Y., Doubleday, 1927.

Commager, Henry Steele. The American Mind. New Haven, Yale University Press, 1950.

"Comment" [on the meaning of the *Dial* award], *The Dial*, LXXII (Jan., 1922), 116–18.

"Comment" [on the anti-Puritan literary movement], *The Dial*, LXXII (Feb., 1922), 232–34.

"Comment" [on the Dial award to T. S. Eliot], *The Dial*, LXXIII (Dec., 1922), 685–87.

"Comment" [on kinds of literary motivation], *The Dial*, LXXV (Sept., 1923), 311–12.

"Comment" [on the *Dial* award to Van Wyck Brooks], *The Dial*, LXXVI (Jan., 1924), 96–97.

Cowley, Malcolm. Exile's Return: A Narrative of Ideals. New York, Norton, 1934.

—— Exile's Return: A Literary Odyssey of the 1920s. New York, The Viking Press, 1951.

Cowley, Malcolm, ed. After the Genteel Tradition. New York, Norton, 1937.

Cowley, Malcolm, and Smith, Bernard, eds. Books That Changed Our Minds. New York, Doubleday, 1939.

Criticism in America, Its Function and Status: Essays by Irving Babbitt, W. C. Brownell, Ernest Boyd, T. S. Eliot, H. L. Mencken, Stuart P. Sherman, J. E. Spingarn, and George E. Woodberry. New York, Harcourt Brace, 1924.

Croly, Herbert. The Promise of American Life. New York, Macmillan, 1911.

—— Willard Straight. New York, Macmillan, 1924.

Cummings, E. E. "T. S. Eliot," *The Dial*, LXVIII (June, 1920), 781–84.

Curti, Merle. The Growth of American Thought. 2d ed. New York, Harper, 1951.

Dell, Floyd. Intellectual Vagabondage: An Apology for the Intelligentsia. New York, Doran, 1926.

Dorfman, Joseph M. The Economic Mind in American Civilization. 3 vols. New York, The Viking Press, 1949. Vol. III.

—— Thorstein Veblen and His America. New York, The Viking Press, 1934.

Dupee, F. W. "The Americanism of Van Wyck Brooks," *The Partisan Review*, VI (Summer, 1939), 69–85. Reprinted in *The Partisan Reader*. New York, The Dial Press, 1946.

Eastman, Max. "Clarifying the Light," *The Liberator*, IV (June, 1921), 5–7.

—— "Inspiration or Leadership," *The Liberator*, IV (August, 1921), 7–9.

Edman, Irwin. "Making the Mind Fit the Times," *The Nation*, CXVI (Jan. 18, 1922), 75.

Egbert, Donald Drew, and Persons, Stow, eds. Socialism and American Life. 2 vols. Princeton, Princeton University Press, 1952.

"The Epic of Dullness," *The Nation*, CXI (Nov. 10, 1920), 536–37.

Ervine, St. John. "Literary Taste in America," *The New Republic*, XXIV (Oct. 6, 1920), 144–47.

Filler, Louis. Randolph Bourne. Washington, D.C., American Council of Public Affairs, 1943.

Fleming, Denna Frank. The United States and World Organization, 1920–1933. New York, Columbia University Press, 1938.

Fletcher, John Gould. Life Is My Song. New York, Farrar and Rinehart, 1937.

—— "An Ultra-Modern Poet" [a review of Job le Pauvre by Jean de Bosschère] *The Freeman*, VII (April 11, 1923), 116–17.

Forster, E. M. Goldsworthy Lowes Dickinson. New York, Harcourt Brace, 1934.

Frank, Waldo. Our America. New York, Boni and Liveright, 1919.

*The Freeman*, I–VIII (March 17, 1920–March 5, 1924).

The Freeman Book: Typical Editorials, Essays, Critiques and Other Selections from the Eight Volumes of the *Freeman*, 1920–1924. New York, Huebsch, 1924.

Fuller, Henry B. "Monsieur France's Opinions," *The Freeman*, V (Aug. 16, 1922), 546–47.

Galantière, Lewis. "A French Essayist" [a review of the complete works of Marcel Schwob], *The Freeman*, V (Jan. 14, 1922), 330–32.

Gannett, Lewis W. "Lost and Found" [a criticism of an article, "The Mind of Anatole France," in "Letters to the Editors"], *The Freeman*, I (July 21, 1920), 447.

Gardiner, H. N. [Review of] "The Mind in the Making" *American Historical Review*, XXVII (July, 1922), 767–69.

Garrison, Frank W., ed. Letters from Albert Jay Nock to Edmund C. Evans, Mrs. Edmund C. Evans, and Ellen Winsor. Caldwell, Idaho, The Caxton Printers, 1949.

Geiger, George Raymond. The Philosophy of Henry George. New York, Macmillan, 1933.

George, Henry. Progress and Poverty. Fiftieth Anniversary ed. New York, Robert Schalkenbach Foundation, 1931.

"God's County" [a review of Main Street], *The New Republic*, XXV (Dec. 1, 1920), 20–21.

Gregory, Alyse. "A Feminine Jean-Christophe" [a review of L'Ame Enchantée, Vol. I, Annette et Sylvie, by Romain Rolland], *The Freeman*, VII (March 14, 1923), 21–22.

—— "Sherwood Anderson," *The Dial*, LXXV (Sept., 1923), 243–46.

Griffin, Constance M. Henry Blake Fuller: A Critical Biography. Philadelphia, University of Pennsylvania Press, 1939.

Grimes, Alan Pendleton. The Political Liberalism of the New York "Nation": 1865–1932. Chapel Hill, University of North Carolina Press, 1953.

Hoffman, Frederick J. Freudianism and the Literary Mind. Baton Rouge, Louisiana State University Press, 1945.

—— "Philistine and Puritan in the 1920's: An Example of the Misuse of the American Past," *American Quarterly*, I (Fall, 1949), 247–63.

—— The Twenties. New York, The Viking Press, 1955.

Hoffman, Frederick J., Allen, Charles, and Ulrich, Carolyn F. The Little Magazine. Princeton, Princeton University Press, 1946.

Hofstadter, Richard. The Age of Reform. New York, Knopf, 1955.

—— Social Darwinism in American Thought. Philadelphia, University of Pennsylvania Press, 1944.

Howe, Frederic C. The Confessions of a Reformer. New York, Scribner, 1925.

—— Privilege and Democracy in America. New York, Scribner, 1916.

Howe, M. A. de Wolfe, ed. John Jay Chapman and His Letters. Boston, Houghton Mifflin, 1937.

Jones, Howard Mumford. The Bright Medusa. Urbana, University of Illinois Press, 1952.

Josephson, Matthew. Life Among the Surrealists. New York, Holt, Rinehart and Winston, 1962.

Karsner, David. Debs: His Authorized Life and Letters. New York, Boni and Liveright, 1919.

Kemler, Edgar. The Irreverent Mr. Mencken. Boston, Little, Brown, 1950.

Kirk, Russell. The Conservative Mind: From Burke to Santayana. Chicago, Henry Regnery, 1953.

Klein, Lawrence R.. The Keynesian Revolution. New York, Macmillan, 1947.

Kunitz, Stanley, and Haycraft, Howard, eds. Twentieth Century American Authors. New York, Wilson, 1924.

La Follette, Suzanne. Art in America. New York, Harper, 1929.

—— Concerning Women. New York, Albert and Charles Boni, 1926.

Laidler, Harry Wellington. A History of Socialist Thought. New York, Crowell, 1927.

Lanux, Pierre de. "A Poet of a New Democracy" [a review of Chants du Désespéré by Charles Vildrac], *The Freeman*, III (Aug. 10, 1921), 522–23.

Laski, Harold J. Authority in the Modern State. New Haven, Yale University Press, 1919.

Lerner, Max. "Randolph Bourne and Two Generations," *Twice a Year*, Nos. 5–6 (1940–1941), 54–78.

Lewis, Sinclair. From Main Street to Stockholm: Letters of Sinclair Lewis, 1919–1930. Ed. with an Introduction by Harrison Smith. New York, Harcourt Brace, 1952.

Lewisohn, Ludwig. The Creative Life. New York, Boni and Liveright, 1924.

—— Up Stream: An American Chronicle. New York, Boni and Liveright, 1922.

—— ed. A Modern Book of Criticism. Modern Library ed. New York, Random House, 1919.

Lovett, Robert Morss. All Our Years. New York, The Viking Press, 1948.

—— "An American Morality," *The Dial*, LXIX (Sept., 1920), 293–99.

—— "The Promise of Sherwood Anderson," *The Dial*, LXXII (Jan., 1922), 79–83.

—— "The Novels of Madame Colette," *The Freeman*, VI (Dec. 20, 1922), 345–47; VI (Dec. 27, 1922), 370–72.

McCallum, R. B. Public Opinion and the Last Peace. New York, Oxford University Press, 1944.

Macdougal, Allan Ross, ed. Letters of Edna St. Vincent Millay. New York, Harper, 1952.

Macy, John. The Spirit of American Literature. New York, Doubleday, Page, 1913.

"Main Street in Fiction," *The New Republic*, XXV (Jan. 12, 1921), 183–84.

Mantoux, Etienne. The Carthaginian Peace; or, The Economic Consequences of Mr. Keynes. New York, Scribner, 1952.

Marshall, James. "The Anti-Semitic Problem in America" [a reply to Albert Jay Nock], *The Atlantic Monthly*, CLXVII (Aug., 1941), 144–49.

Martin, Dorothy. "The Countess de Noailles," *The Freeman*, VI (Sept. 20, 1922), 34–36; VI (Sept. 27, 1922), 56–59.

Mason, Daniel Gregory. Music in My Time and Other Reminiscences. New York, Macmillan, 1938.

Mellquist, Jerome, and Wiese, Lucie, eds. Paul Rosenfeld: Voyager in the Arts. New York, Creative Age Press, 1948.

Mencken, H. L. "The Literary Capital of the United States." American Literary Supplement to *The Nation* (London), XXVII (April 17, 1920), 90–92.

Millet, Fred B. Contemporary American Authors, a Critical Survey and 219 Bio-bibliographies. New York, Harcourt Brace, 1940.

"The Mind of Anatole France," *The Freeman*, I (July 7, 1920), 391–92.

Mizener, Arthur. The Far Side of Paradise. Boston, Houghton Mifflin, 1951.

—— "Fitzgerald in the Twenties," *The Partisan Review*, XVII (Jan., 1950), 7–23.

"Moon-Calf on the Mississippi," *The Nation*, CXI (Dec. 8, 1920), 670–72.

Moore, Marianne. "The Dial," *Life and Letters Today*, XXVII (Dec., 1940), 175–83; XXVIII (Jan., 1941), 3–9.

Morris, Lloyd. Postscript to Yesterday: America the Last Fifty Years. New York, Random House, 1947.

Muir, Edwin. Autobiography. London, The Hogarth Press, 1954.

—— Latitudes. New York, Huebsch, 1924.

—— Transition: Essays on Contemporary Literature. New York, The Viking Press, 1926.

—— We Moderns: Enigmas and Guesses. New York, Knopf, 1920.

Mumford, Lewis. The Golden Day. New York, Boni and Liveright, 1926.

—— Sticks and Stones, A Study of American Architecture and Civilization. New York, Boni and Liveright, 1924.

Munson, Gorham B. "Van Wyck Brooks: His Sphere and His Encroachments," *The Dial*, LXXVIII (Jan., 1925), 28–42.

—— An exchange with John Brooks Wheelwright on the meaning of a literary secession. *Secession*, No. 4 (Jan., 1923), 29–30.

—— "The Mechanics for a Literary Secession," *S4N*. Third Anniversary ed. (Nov., 1922).

Neilson, Francis. Modern Man and the Liberal Arts: Critical Essays. New York, Robert Schalkenbach Foundation, 1947.

—— How Diplomats Make War. 2d ed. New York, Huebsch, 1920.

Neilson, Francis. My Life in Two Worlds. 2 vols. Appleton, Wis., Nelson, 1953.
—— The Old Freedom. New York, Huebsch, 1919.
—— The Story of "The Freeman." Published under Special Grant as a Supplement to *The American Journal of Economics and Sociology*, VI (Oct., 1946).
Nevins, Allan. American Press Opinion, Washington to Coolidge: A Documentary Record of Editorial Leadership and Criticism, 1785–1927. New York, Heath, 1928.
Nock, Albert Jay. The Book of Journeyman: Essays from the New Freeman. New York, Publishers of the New Freeman, 1930.
—— Henry George. New York, William Morrow, 1939.
—— Jefferson. Washington, D.C., National Home Library Foundation, 1926.
—— "The Jewish Problem in America," *The Atlantic Monthly*, CLXVII (June, 1941), 699–706; CLXVIII (July, 1941), 67–76.
—— A Journal of Forgotten Days, 1934–35. Hinsdale, Ill., Henry Regnery, 1948.
—— A Journal of These Days. New York, William Morrow, 1934.
—— Memoirs of a Superfluous Man. New York, Harper, 1943.
—— Our Enemy, The State. New York, William Morrow, 1935.
—— "The Things That Are Caesar's," *The American Magazine*, LXXI (Dec., 1910–April, 1911), 147–58, 302–8, 450–55, 631–36, 714–19; LXXII (May, 1911–Aug., 1911), 76–87, 221–30, 335–38, 428–31.
—— "The West Faces the Land Question," *The Century Magazine*, LXXIII (1917–18), 295–301.
Nock, Francis J., ed. Selected Letters of Albert Jay Nock. Collected and ed. by Francis J. Nock, and with "Memories of Albert Jay Nock" by Ruth Robinson. Caldwell, Idaho, The Caxton Printers, 1962.
Oppenheimer, Franz. The State. Translated by John M. Gitterman. New York, The Vanguard Press, 1926.
O'Sullivan, Vincent. "Guillaume Apollinaire," *The Freeman*, II (Dec. 29, 1920), 370–72.
"The Passing of the Freeman," *The New Republic*, XXXVIII (March 5, 1924), 33–34.
A Petition to the Congress of the United States for an Inquiry into the Pro-German Propaganda of Albert Jay Nock. A pamphlet

published by Alexander Kadison, 35 Fifth Avenue, New York,
April 14, 1947.

Pound, Ezra. "Paris Letter," *The Dial*, LXXII (June, 1922), 625–29.

—— Patria Mia. Chicago, Ralph Fletcher Seymour, 1950.

Rascoe, Burton. A Bookman's Daybook. Ed. and with an Introduction by C. Hartley Grattan. New York, Horace Liveright,
1929.

Read, Leonard. "From the Publisher," *The Freeman*, V (July,
1954), 5.

"The Return of Anatole France," *The Freeman*, I (Aug. 4, 1920),
485–86.

"A Reviewer's Notebook" [on André Gide and a school of letters],
*The Freeman*, II (Oct. 27, 1920), 166–67.

Rosenfeld, Paul. Men Seen. New York, The Dial Press, 1925.

—— Port of New York, Harcourt Brace, 1924.

—— "Randolph Bourne," *The Dial*, LXXV (Dec., 1923), 545–60.

—— "Sherwood Anderson," *The Dial*, LXXII (Jan., 1922), 29–42.

Russell, Bertrand. Proposed Roads to Freedom: Socialism, Anarchism, Syndicalism. New York, Henry Holt, 1919.

Sanborn, Pitts. "A Talk with Anatole France," *The Freeman*, II
(Feb. 9, 1921), 514–15.

Santayana, George. Character and Opinion in the United States.
New York, Scribner, 1920.

—— "Marginal Notes on 'Civilization in the United States,'" *The
Dial*, LXXII (June, 1922), 553–58.

—— Winds of Doctrine: Studies in Contemporary Opinion. New
York, Scribner, 1926.

Sedgwick, Ellery. The Happy Profession. Boston, Little, Brown,
1946.

Seldes, Gilbert. "Ulysses," *The Nation*, CXV (Aug. 30, 1922),
211–12.

Sherman, Stuart P. Americans. New York, Scribner, 1922.

—— The Genius of America. New York, Scribner, 1923.

—— "Is There Anything to Be Said for Literary Tradition?"
*The Bookman*, LII (Oct., 1920), 108–12.

—— "The National Genius," *The Atlantic Monthly*, CXXVII
(Jan., 1921), 1–10.

—— On Contemporary Literature. New York, Henry Holt, 1917.

"Shorter Notices" [a short review of Monsieur Bergeret in Paris by Anatole France], *The Freeman*, V (Aug. 23, 1922), 574. Signed C.C.

Slosson, Preston William. The Great Crusade and After, 1914–1928. New York, Macmillan, 1930.

Spencer, Herbert. The Man Versus the State. With an Introduction by Albert Jay Nock. Caldwell, Idaho, The Caxton Printers, 1940.

Spingarn, Joel E. The New Criticism: A Lecture Delivered at Columbia University, March 9, 1910. New York, Columbia University Press, 1911.

Stearns, Harold E. America and the Young Intellectual. New York, Doran, 1921.

—— The Street I Know. New York, Lee Furman, 1935.

Stearns Harold E., ed. Civilization in the United States: An Inquiry by Thirty Americans. New York, Harcourt Brace, 1922.

Steffens, Lincoln. The Autobiography of Lincoln Steffens. 2 vols. New York, The Literary Guild, 1931.

—— "Interesting People: Joseph Fels." *The American Magazine*, LXX (Oct., 1910), 744–45.

Stuart, Henry Logan. "A Pagan Morality" [a review of Le Grand Ecart by Jean Cocteau], *The Freeman*, VIII (Oct. 3, 1923), 91–92.

Sullivan, Mark. Our Times: The United States, 1900–1925. New York, Scribner, 1926.

Swift, Louis F. The Yankee of the Yards. Written in collaboration with Arthur Van Vlissingen, Jr. Chicago, Shaw, 1927.

Tawney, R. H. The Acquisitive Society. New York, Harcourt, Brace and Howe, 1920.

Thirwell, John C., ed. The Selected Letters of William Carlos Williams. Ed. and with an Introduction by John C. Thirwell. New York, McDowell, Obolensky, 1957.

Trilling, Lionel. The Liberal Imagination. New York, The Viking Press, 1950.

Van Doren, Carl. "The Fruits of the Frontier," *The Nation*, CXI (Aug. 14, 1920), 189.

Van Loon, Hendrik Willem. "Achilles," *The Dial*, LXXII (Feb., 1922), 201–2.

Villard, Henry. Memoirs of Henry Villard, Journalist and Financier, 1835–1900. 2 vols. Boston, Houghton Mifflin, 1904.

Villard, Oswald Garrison. Fighting Years: Memoirs of a Liberal Editor. New York, Harcourt Brace, 1939.

Weber, Brom, ed. The Letters of Hart Crane. New York, Hermitage House, 1952.

Wecter, Dixon. The Saga of American Society: A Record of Social Aspiration, 1607–1937. New York, Scribner, 1937.

White, Morton Gabriel. Social Thought in America: The Revolt against Formalism. New York, The Viking Press, 1949.

Whitlock, Brand. Forty Years of It. New York, Appleton, 1914.

—— The Letters and Journals of Brand Whitlock. Edited by Allan Nevins. New York, Appleton-Century, 1936.

Williams, William Carlos. The Autobiography of William Carlos Williams. New York, Random House, 1951.

Wilson, Edmund. Discordant Encounters: Plays and Dialogues. New York, Albert and Charles Boni, 1926.

—— "Imaginary Conversations: Mr. Van Wyck Brooks and Mr. Scott Fitzgerald," *The New Republic*, XXXVIII (April 30, 1924), 249–54.

—— The Shores of Light: A Literary Chronicle of the Twenties and Thirties. New York, Farrar, Strauss and Young, 1952.

—— "The Pilgrimage of Van Wyck Brooks," *The New Republic*, XLII (May 6, 1925), 283–86.

—— "Ulysses," *The New Republic*, XXXI (July 5, 1922), 164–66.

Wilson, Woodrow. The New Freedom: A Call for the Emancipation of the Generous Energies of a People. New York, Doubleday, Page, 1921.

Wood, Plysted. Magazines in the United States: Their Social and Economic Influence. New York, Ronald Press, 1949.

Young, Arthur Nichols. The Single Tax Movement in the United States. Princeton, Princeton University Press, 1916.

Zabel, Morton Dauwen, ed. Literary Opinion in America. New York, Harper, 1951.

Zeitlin, Jacob, and Woodbridge, Homer. Life and Letters of Stuart P. Sherman. New York, Farrar and Rinehart, 1929.

Zilboorg, Gregory. "A Modern Jeremiah" [Romain Rolland], *The Freeman*, I (May 5, 1920), 182–83.

—— "Romain Rolland and Russia," in "Letters to the Editors," *The Freeman*, I (April 7, 1920), 82.

# Index